Repair Your Credit: Remove Errors, Pay Down Debt, Rebuild Score

Torzen Kalrix

REPAIR YOUR CREDIT: REMOVE ERRORS, PAY DOWN DEBT, REBUILD SCORE

First edition. February 11, 2026.

ISBN: 979-8233887727

Written by Torzen Kalrix.

Table of Contents

Welcome to Your Credit Comeback

Let me tell you about the worst day of my adult life.

I was sitting in a car dealership, cocky as hell, ready to drive off in a slightly used sedan that would finally replace my rolling disaster of a vehicle. The salesman had that fake smile plastered on his face as he ran my credit. Then his expression changed. You know that look? The one that says "oh buddy, we have a problem."

My credit score was 537.

Five. Thirty. Seven.

I didn't even know scores went that low. I thought 600 was rock bottom. Turns out, I was an overachiever in all the wrong ways. The salesman actually laughed - not with me, at me - and said I'd need a co-signer or a 23% interest rate. Twenty-three percent. On a used Honda Civic.

I left that dealership on foot, took the bus home, and spent the entire night staring at my credit report like it was written in ancient hieroglyphics. Collections I'd forgotten about. Late payments from three years ago. An account I'd never even opened. It was a disaster movie, and I was the star.

That's when I got mad. Really mad.

See, I wasn't some reckless spender. I worked hard. I paid my bills... mostly on time... okay, sometimes late, but still. The system felt rigged, and nobody had ever taught me the rules. So I did what any stubborn person would do - I became obsessed with figuring this whole credit thing out.

Six months later, my score hit 720. A year after that, I was over 780.

No credit repair company. No magic pills. Just information that apparently nobody wants to share unless you're paying them three grand for it. And that's exactly why I wrote this book - because that information should be free, and your credit score shouldn't determine your worth or your future.

What You're About to Learn

This book is your battle plan for credit domination. We're starting from the ground up because most people don't even know how to read their credit reports. **Chapter 1** gets you fluent in credit-speak - what those three bureaus actually do, how to get your reports for free, and what all those codes mean. Spoiler alert: it's not as complicated as they want you to think.

Chapter 2 breaks down your actual credit score. We're talking FICO versus VantageScore, the five factors that make or break your number, and busting myths that are probably costing you points right now. You'll finally understand why your score dropped 30 points because you checked your own credit (just kidding, that's a myth we'll bust).

Then we get tactical. **Chapter 3** teaches you to hunt for errors like a detective with a grudge. Most credit reports have mistakes - I'm talking wrong addresses, phantom accounts, debts that aren't yours. You'll learn to spot them all.

Chapter 4 is your dispute bootcamp. I'm handing you the exact process for challenging errors with credit bureaus, the magic words that get results, and what to do when they try to brush you off. The Fair Credit Reporting Act is your new best friend, and I'll show you how to weaponize it legally.

Chapter 5 takes it up a notch with advanced strategies. This is where we get sneaky - disputing directly with creditors, using verification methods that make them sweat, and knowing when to escalate. These are the tactics that separate amateurs from credit ninjas.

Chapter 6 might be my favorite because we're tackling those terrifying collection accounts. I'll show you how to negotiate pay-for-delete agreements, validate debts so collection agencies have to prove they own what they claim, and handle those zombie debts that keep rising from the grave. Collections aren't as powerful as they seem once you know their weaknesses.

Chapter 7 is all about actually paying down debt without living on ramen for five years. The avalanche method, the snowball method, budgeting that doesn't make you miserable - it's all here. Plus negotiation tactics for lowering your interest rates because yes, that's totally possible.

Chapter 8 reveals the credit utilization secret that changed my life. This one factor can boost your score fast if you play it right. I'll show you the 30% rule, how to game the system with payment timing, and tricks for lowering utilization without actually paying off everything.

Chapter 9 is about building positive history fast. Authorized user strategies, secured cards that actually work, credit builder loans - we're constructing a solid credit foundation so you never end up in this mess again.

Chapter 10 is for anyone recovering from the big stuff - bankruptcy, foreclosure, repossession. Yes, you can come back from these. I'll show you exactly how, with realistic timelines and actionable steps.

Finally, **Chapter 11** makes sure you stay winning. Credit monitoring, annual reviews, identity theft protection, and habits that keep your score high forever. Because fixing your credit once is good. Never having to fix it again is better.

Here's the Deal

I wrote this book in the same casual, no-nonsense way I'd explain it to my best friend over coffee. No financial jargon unless absolutely necessary. No corporate doublespeak. Just straight talk about how credit really works and how to make it work for you.

You don't need to be a finance expert. You don't need thousands of dollars. You just need this information and the willingness to take action. Some of these strategies work in days. Others take months. But all of them work if you actually do them.

Your credit score isn't a life sentence. It's not a measure of your intelligence or your character. It's just a number that someone decided matters, and since it does matter for getting apartments, loans, and decent interest rates, we might as well master it.

So let's do this. Let's turn your credit from a source of anxiety into a source of power. Ready? Let's go.

Chapter 1: Understanding Your Credit Report

Remember that time you tried to read your credit report and felt like you accidentally opened a document written in Klingon? Yeah, me too. The first time I stared at mine, I saw more abbreviations than a military memo and enough codes to crack the Da Vinci Code sequel. Equifax, Experian, TransUnion - they sounded like evil corporations from a sci-fi movie, and honestly, they kind of act like it too. But here's the secret they don't want you to know: once you understand what you're looking at, these reports are just organized lists of your financial history. That's it. No magic. No mystery. Just data that you absolutely need to understand because it's controlling your financial life whether you like it or not.

This chapter provides a comprehensive foundation for understanding credit reports and the three major credit bureaus that compile them. You will learn how to obtain your free annual credit reports from Equifax, Experian, and TransUnion, as mandated by federal law. We will decode the various sections of your credit report, including personal information, credit accounts, payment history, and public records. Additionally, this chapter explains the codes, abbreviations, and terminology used throughout credit reports, enabling you to identify which information impacts your creditworthiness and which elements require your immediate attention.

1.1 The Three Major Credit Bureaus and Their Roles

Let's start with the three gatekeepers of your financial reputation: Equifax, Experian, and TransUnion. These aren't lenders. They don't give you money, approve your loans, or decide whether you deserve that shiny new credit card. Yet somehow, they hold terrifying power over whether you get approved, what interest rate you pay, and sometimes even whether you get a job or an apartment.

After 20 years in this field, I can tell you something important right up front: credit bureaus are not judges. They are more like filing cabinets with a serious attitude problem. Their job is to collect information, organize it, and sell versions of it to lenders. That's it. Understanding this alone will save you a lot of unnecessary fear.

Who Are These Companies, Really?

The three major credit bureaus are private, for-profit companies. They are not government agencies, even though they often feel like they should be. Each one maintains its own database of consumer credit information, which is why your credit reports are never identical across all three.

Here's a quick breakdown:

- **Equifax** – One of the oldest bureaus, founded in 1899. Yes, 1899. Credit reporting started before sliced bread, which explains a lot. Equifax tends to be heavily used by mortgage lenders.

- **Experian** – Originally based in the UK, Experian is now the largest credit bureau globally. They're big in auto loans and credit cards.

- **TransUnion** – The youngest of the three, founded in 1968. TransUnion is commonly used for tenant screenings and consumer credit products.

Each bureau collects data independently. Think of them as three nosy neighbors who all watch your house, but from different angles and with different notebooks. They talk to some of the same lenders, but not all of them, and they don't always write things down the same way.

What Information Do Credit Bureaus Collect?

Credit bureaus gather information from data furnishers, which include banks, credit card companies, auto lenders, mortgage lenders, student loan servicers, and collection agencies. These companies voluntarily report information about your accounts.

That last part matters. Reporting is voluntary, but accuracy is not. Once a company chooses to report, they are legally required to report correctly.

Here's what the bureaus typically collect:

- Personal identifying information (name variations, addresses, Social Security number fragments, date of birth)
- Credit accounts (credit cards, loans, mortgages)
- Payment history (on-time, late, missed)
- Credit limits and balances
- Collections and charge-offs
- Public records (bankruptcy, judgments where applicable)

What they do not collect:

- Your income
- Your bank account balances

- Your race, religion, or political views

Your Netflix password, no matter how much it feels like they know everything else

Why Your Reports Differ Across Bureaus

One of the most common questions I hear is, "Why does Experian show something that TransUnion doesn't?" Short answer: because they can.

Not all lenders report to all three bureaus. Some report to one, some to two, some to all three. On top of that, reporting timing differs. One bureau might update today, another next week. This leads to:

- Accounts appearing on one report but not another
- Slightly different balances
- Different payment statuses
- Different dispute outcomes

This is also why you can't fix credit by looking at just one report. I've seen people clean up Experian perfectly and then get blindsided by TransUnion six months later.

Professional rule: always work with all three reports. Anything less is gambling.

What Role Credit Bureaus Actually Play

Let's clear up a huge misconception. Credit bureaus do not decide if information is true. They don't investigate accounts proactively. They don't double-check balances. They don't ask lenders, "Hey, are you sure about this late payment?"

Their role is passive:

- Receive data

- Store data
- Share data
- Investigate disputes only when legally required

Think of them like a bulletin board. If someone pins a wrong notice on it, the board doesn't argue. It just holds the paper until someone forces a correction.

This is why errors are so common. And it's why you are the quality control department for your own credit.

How Lenders Use Credit Bureau Data

When you apply for credit, a lender pulls a report (or reports) from one or more bureaus. They may also pull a credit score generated from that bureau's data. Based on that snapshot, they decide:

- Approve or deny
- Interest rate
- Credit limit
- Loan terms

Important detail: lenders choose which bureau to pull, not you. You don't get to say, "Hey, my TransUnion looks better, use that one." If that were allowed, this book would be much shorter.

This is also why a single error can cost you real money. A wrong late payment can mean:

- Higher interest rates
- Larger deposits
- Denied applications
- Lost opportunities you never even hear about

- The Credit Bureaus Make Money From Your Data

This part usually annoys people, and honestly, it should. Credit bureaus make money by selling access to your credit information to lenders, insurers, landlords, and employers (with permission). You are the product.

You don't pay them directly, but they profit from your financial behavior. This is why they're not exactly motivated to proactively clean up mistakes unless you force the issue through proper channels.

Understanding this dynamic is empowering. It explains why the system feels indifferent. It's not personal. It's business.

Why Knowing Their Role Changes Everything

Once you stop seeing credit bureaus as authority figures and start seeing them as data processors, your mindset shifts. You stop feeling helpless and start acting strategically.

Instead of:

- "They ruined my credit"

You think:

- "They are reporting incorrect data, and I know the legal process to fix it"

That shift is the foundation of credit repair.

In the chapters ahead, we'll go step by step through:

- How to get your reports from all three bureaus
- How to read them without wanting to cry
- How to identify what actually matters
- How to force corrections using the law, not frustration

For now, just remember this: the credit bureaus work for the system, not for you. That's why you have to advocate for yourself. Once you do, they're a lot less scary than they look on paper.

1.2 How to Request Your Free Annual Credit Reports

Let me save you about three hours of Googling, two mild panic attacks, and at least one moment where you almost typed your Social Security number into a sketchy website. There is exactly one official way to get your free credit reports, and once you know it, this process becomes boring in the best possible way.

By law, you are entitled to one free credit report every 12 months from each of the three major credit bureaus. That's three reports total. Not a trial. Not a promo. Not a "free unless you forget to cancel." Just free.

I've walked thousands of people through this over the last 20 years, and here's the truth: most people don't mess this up because it's hard. They mess it up because they rush, click ads, or don't know what to expect.

We're not doing that.

The Only Legitimate Website You Should Use

The official site authorized by federal law is:

- AnnualCreditReport.com

That's it. Burn it into your memory. Bookmark it. Tattoo it on your soul if necessary.

If a site asks for a credit card to "unlock" your free report, close the tab. If it promises your score will "skyrocket instantly," run. You're not shopping for motivation. You're collecting raw data.

This site does not give you your credit score. That's intentional. Right now, you're focused on reports, not scores. Scores come later.

What You'll Need Before You Start

Before you sit down to request your reports, grab the following:

- Your full legal name
- Social Security number
- Date of birth
- Current address
- Any previous addresses from the last two years

Credit bureaus use address history to verify identity. If you've moved recently and can't remember how you formatted an old apartment address, expect a hiccup. That's normal.

Pro tip from experience: use exact address formatting from old bills or tax documents if you can. "St." versus "Street" has ruined many otherwise peaceful afternoons.

Step-by-Step: Requesting Your Reports Online

Here's how the process actually works:

- Go to AnnualCreditReport.com
- Click "Request your free credit reports"
- Enter your personal information
- Select which bureaus you want (always select all three)
- Answer identity verification questions
- View or download your reports

Those identity questions will feel oddly personal. Things like:

- Which lender issued your auto loan?
- What street have you lived on?

- Which of these accounts looks familiar?

They're pulled from your credit file. If none of the answers apply, that's okay. There's usually an option for "none of the above." Guessing wrong too many times can lock you out temporarily, so don't rush.

Online vs Mail vs Phone: Which Is Best?

- You have three options. Here's the honest breakdown.
- Online (Best Option)
- Instant access
- Easiest to review
- Can download and save PDFs
- Most efficient for disputes later

Mail (Slow but Sometimes Necessary)

- Used if online verification fails
- Requires proof of identity
- Takes 2–3 weeks
- Good backup option

Phone (I Do Not Recommend)

- Limited visibility
- Hard to review details
- No easy paper trail

If you must use mail, here's what you'll need to send:

- Completed request form (available on the site)

- Copy of government-issued ID
- Copy of proof of address (utility bill or bank statement)

Mailing address is provided directly on the official site. Do not trust addresses found elsewhere.

How Often Should You Pull Your Reports?

Legally, you get one free report per bureau every 12 months. Strategically, you have options.

You can:

- Pull all three at once for a full audit
- Stagger them every four months for ongoing monitoring

When I'm actively repairing credit, I pull all three at once. I want to see the full battlefield before making any moves. Later, when things are clean, staggering makes sense.

During special periods (like the pandemic), free weekly reports were temporarily allowed. Those rules can change, so always check the site for current availability.

What to Do Immediately After You Get Your Reports

This is where most people mess up. They skim, feel overwhelmed, and close the tab. Don't do that.

Instead:

- Save each report as a PDF
- Name the files clearly (Example: Experian_Jan2026.pdf)
- Print them if possible
- Grab a pen or highlighter

Your job right now is not to fix anything. Your job is to observe.

You're looking for:

- Accounts you don't recognize
- Late payments that seem wrong
- Balances that look off
- Accounts that should be closed but aren't
- Negative items older than they should be

We'll go deep on how to analyze this in the next section, but step one is simply having clean copies you can reference.

What If You're Denied Access?

This happens more than people admit, especially if:

- You've moved a lot
- You recently froze your credit
- Your file is thin or inactive

If online access fails:

- Switch to mail request
- Include clear copies of ID
- Be patient

This is not a red flag. It's an inconvenience. We deal with it and move on.

One Rule I Beg You to Follow

Never rely on:

- Credit monitoring apps
- Bank summaries
- "Credit snapshots"
- Third-party summaries

Those tools are fine later. Right now, you need full, unfiltered reports directly from the source. Anything else is like diagnosing a car problem using a blurry photo.

Once you have your reports, you're officially in control. Everything else in this book depends on this step, so don't rush it, don't outsource it, and don't skip it.

You can't fix what you haven't seen.

1.3 Reading and Interpreting Your Credit Report

This is the moment where most people open their credit report, scroll for about twelve seconds, feel their soul leave their body, and quietly decide to "come back to this later." Totally normal. Credit reports are not designed to be friendly, intuitive, or emotionally supportive. They are designed for lenders, not humans.

But after 20 years of reading these things for a living, I can promise you this: once you know the layout, a credit report is actually predictable. Dry, yes. Confusing at first, absolutely. But not complicated. Think instruction manual, not ancient prophecy.

Let's walk through it together like normal people.

First Rule: You're Not Reading, You're Auditing

When you read a credit report, you're not reading it like a book. You're scanning it like an accountant with trust issues. Your goal is to identify:

- What's accurate
- What's inaccurate
- What's outdated
- What's hurting your score

You are not judging yourself. You are judging the data.

Grab a pen. Or a highlighter. Or open a notes app. You're about to mark things up.

Section 1: Personal Information

This section usually comes first, and it looks harmless. Names, addresses, employers, date of birth.

Here's what to know: this section does not directly affect your score. But errors here can cause serious problems indirectly.

Check for:

- Misspelled names
- Name variations you never used
- Incorrect Social Security number fragments
- Addresses you don't recognize
- Old employers that aren't yours

Why this matters: incorrect personal info can link your report to someone else's accounts. This is how "that's not my debt" stories begin.

If you see minor variations (like "Mike" vs "Michael"), don't panic. If you see a completely unfamiliar name or address, circle it. We'll deal with it later.

Section 2: Credit Accounts (Trade Lines)

This is the heart of the report and where most of the damage lives.

Each account listing usually includes:

- Creditor name
- Account type (credit card, auto loan, mortgage, student loan)
- Date opened
- Credit limit or loan amount
- Current balance
- Payment history

- Account status

Go account by account. Slowly. Painfully if necessary.

For each account, ask:

- Is this mine?
- Is the balance accurate?
- Is the status correct (open, closed, paid, charged off)?
- Are the payment dates accurate?

Late payments are usually shown in a grid format with codes like 30, 60, 90. One wrong late payment can tank your score for years. Don't assume they're right.

Professional habit: circle anything negative first. We'll separate "fixable" from "unfortunate but accurate" later.

Section 3: Payment History Details

This is where lenders obsess, and you should too.

Look for:

- Late payments reported incorrectly
- Payments reported late when you paid on time
- Accounts marked "delinquent" that were in deferment or hardship programs
- Closed accounts still reporting monthly late payments

Here's a reality check: payment history is the single most important factor in your credit score. Even one error here matters.

If you ever set up autopay and assumed everything was fine, this is where you find out if that trust was misplaced.

Section 4: Collections and Charge-Offs

This section hurts to read. I know. Take a breath.

Collections usually list:

- Original creditor
- Collection agency
- Date of first delinquency
- Amount owed
- Status (open, paid, settled)

Charge-offs are accounts the lender gave up on but never forgot.

Important truths:

- Paying a collection does not automatically remove it
- Paid charge-offs can still hurt your score
- Dates matter more than balances

Check carefully for:

- Duplicate collections for the same debt
- Collections older than seven years
- Collections that don't belong to you

If you see the same debt listed multiple times, that's a big red flag.

Section 5: Public Records (If Any)

Depending on current reporting rules, this section may be empty. If it's not, it usually includes:

- Bankruptcies
- Tax liens (in limited cases)

Verify:

- Filing dates
- Chapter type
- Status (discharged vs open)

Public records have strict reporting timelines. If they're still showing past their legal limit, they should not be there.

Section 6: Credit Inquiries

This section shows who accessed your credit.

Two types:

- **Hard inquiries** – affect your score
- **Soft inquiries** – do not

Hard inquiries should only appear if you applied for credit. If you see lenders you don't recognize, note them.

Too many hard inquiries in a short time can lower your score, but one or two are normal. Don't overreact here.

How to Mark Your Report Like a Pro

Here's my personal system:

- Circle errors in red

- Highlight negative but accurate items in yellow
- Leave positive accounts alone
- Write notes in the margin

You're building a roadmap, not fixing anything yet.

What Not to Do (Please)

- Don't dispute everything at once
- Don't assume old equals wrong
- Don't panic over every negative item
- Don't rely on summaries or scores yet

Credit repair is not about attacking blindly. It's about precision.

The Goal of This Step

By the end of this process, you should be able to answer:

- What's wrong?
- What's hurting me most?
- What can realistically be fixed?

Once you can see your report clearly, it loses its power to intimidate you. In the next section, we'll decode the weird codes and abbreviations that make these reports look scarier than they are.

For now, congratulations. You just did what most people never do: you actually looked.

1.4 Understanding Credit Report Codes and Abbreviations

If credit reports were written in plain English, this book would be about twelve pages long and we'd all be done by now. Unfortunately, credit bureaus love codes, abbreviations, and cryptic little symbols that make your report look like it was formatted by someone who gets paid per confusion.

The good news? There's no secret meaning here. These codes exist to save space and standardize data across lenders. Once you learn the most common ones, you'll stop feeling lost and start spotting problems fast. After 20 years of reading these things, I don't even "read" credit reports anymore. I scan for patterns and codes. You're about to do the same.

Why These Codes Matter More Than You Think

Every single code on your credit report translates to:

- How risky a lender thinks you are
- Whether an account is helping or hurting you
- Whether information is accurate or disputable

One wrong letter or number can mean the difference between approval and denial. So yes, learning this stuff is boring. But it's boring in the same way wearing a seatbelt is boring. Necessary and effective.

Account Status Codes (The Big Ones)

These codes describe the current condition of an account. Pay close attention here.

Common status codes include:

- **OK / Current** – Account is paid as agreed. Boring. Beautiful.

- **30 / 60 / 90 / 120** – Days late. The higher the number, the worse the damage.

- **CO** – Charge-off. The creditor gave up but the debt still exists.

- **COLL** – Collection. The account was sent to a collection agency.

- **PD / PIF** – Paid or Paid in Full.

- **SETTLED** – Paid for less than owed. Better than unpaid, worse than paid in full.

- **CLOSED** – Account closed (not necessarily bad).

- **DEFAULT** – Account seriously delinquent.

- **REPO** – Repossession.

- **BK** – Bankruptcy-related account.

If an account shows "CLOSED" but still reports late payments every month, that's a red flag. Closed accounts should not continue accumulating damage.

Payment Rating Codes (Sneaky but Powerful)

These codes show how well you paid the account historically. They often appear as letters or numbers.

Common examples:

- **0 / 1** – Paid on time

- **2** – 30 days late

- **3** – 60 days late

- **4** – 90 days late

- **5** – 120+ days late

- **L** – Late
- **G** – Collection
- **B** – No data available

One misreported "3" instead of a "1" can quietly crush your score. Always verify these against your records if something feels off.

Account Type Codes

These tell lenders what kind of debt you have.

Typical abbreviations:

- **REV** – Revolving (credit cards)
- **INST** – Installment (auto loans, personal loans)
- **MTG** – Mortgage
- **STU** – Student loan
- **HELOC** – Home equity line of credit

Why this matters: credit mix impacts your score. Mislabeling an account type can skew how lenders see your profile.

Credit Limit and Balance Codes

You may see abbreviations like:

- **CL** – Credit limit
- **BAL** – Current balance
- **HICR / HILIM** – Highest credit or high limit

If your high limit is reported incorrectly, it can inflate your utilization ratio and lower your score. This happens more often than people realize, especially after credit limit increases.

Date Codes (Where the Real Power Lives)

Dates are everything in credit reporting.

Watch for:

- DOFD – Date of First Delinquency
- Date Opened
- Date Closed
- Date Reported
- Date Last Activity (DLA)

The Date of First Delinquency determines when a negative account must legally fall off your report (usually seven years). If this date is wrong, the account can stay longer than allowed.

This is one of the most important things to verify on your entire report.

Special Comment Codes

These are short notes lenders add. Some are harmless. Some are lethal.

Common examples:

- "Consumer disputes account" – Neutral during dispute, but can affect approvals temporarily
- "Account included in bankruptcy"
- "Transferred to another lender"
- "Paid after charge-off"

Comments can explain inconsistencies, but they can also hide problems. Read them carefully.

Collection-Specific Codes

Collections often use their own shorthand:

- OC – Original Creditor
- CA – Collection Agency
- Placed for collection
- Purchased debt
- Assigned debt

"Purchased" means the collector owns the debt. "Assigned" means they're collecting for someone else. Ownership matters when disputing.

How to Use Codes Strategically

Here's how professionals use codes:

- Spot contradictions (closed but still late)
- Identify wrong account types
- Find incorrect delinquency dates
- Detect duplicate or re-aged accounts
- Build precise disputes instead of emotional ones

When you reference codes directly in disputes, bureaus and creditors take you more seriously. You're speaking their language.

What You Don't Need to Memorize

You do not need to memorize every code on Earth. Focus on:

- Status
- Payment history

- Dates
- Ownership

Everything else is secondary.

The Takeaway

Credit report codes aren't there to trick you. They're there to standardize data. Once you understand them, they stop being scary and start becoming tools.

In the next section, we'll pull everything together by identifying the key sections of your credit report and prioritizing what actually needs your attention first.

1.5 Identifying the Key Sections of Your Credit Report

At this point, you've probably noticed something: your credit report is long. Painfully long. I've seen reports that are three pages and others that are sixty. And here's the dirty secret no one tells you—you do not need to treat every section with equal emotional energy.

One of the biggest mistakes people make is assuming every line on their credit report is equally important. It's not. Some sections barely matter, some matter a lot, and a few can completely wreck your financial life if they're wrong. After 20 years of reviewing these reports, I've learned how to triage them like an ER doctor. Let me show you how to do the same.

The goal here is simple: know where to focus first and where not to waste your sanity.

Section One: Personal Information (Low Score Impact, High Error Risk)

This section usually appears first and includes:

- Name variations
- Current and previous addresses
- Date of birth
- Partial Social Security number
- Employment history

Let's get something straight: this section does not affect your credit score directly. You could have five old addresses listed and still have an 800 score.

So why do we care?

Because errors here can link your file to someone else's accounts. That's how people end up with debts they swear they've never seen before. If you see:

- Names that aren't yours
- Addresses you never lived at
- Employers you never worked for

Flag them. Don't panic. Just mark them. These errors are often fixable and usually handled later in the process.

Section Two: Credit Accounts / Trade Lines (Highest Priority)

This is the most important section of your entire credit report. Full stop.

Trade lines include:

- Credit cards
- Auto loans
- Mortgages
- Student loans
- Personal loans

This section directly affects:

- Payment history
- Credit utilization
- Length of credit history
- Credit mix

In other words, most of your score lives here.

When reviewing trade lines, focus on:

- Account status (open, closed, charged off)
- Payment history accuracy
- Balances vs credit limits
- Dates opened and closed

If you're short on time, this is where you spend it. Errors here cost real money.

Section Three: Payment History Details (Silent Score Killers)

Sometimes payment history is baked into the trade lines. Sometimes it's broken out separately in grids or timelines.

This section shows:

- On-time payments
- Late payments by month
- Severity of delinquency

Here's the hard truth: one incorrect late payment can drop your score 40–100 points. I've seen it more times than I can count.

Pay extra attention to:

- Accounts marked late during hardship programs
- Payments reported late after account closure
- Random late months that don't match your records

This section is boring, repetitive, and incredibly important.

Section Four: Collections and Charge-Offs (Emotional Damage Section)

This section gets all the attention because it hurts the most to look at. But don't let feelings override logic.

Collections and charge-offs include:

- Collection agency accounts
- Charged-off credit cards or loans
- Medical collections
- Utility collections

What to prioritize here:

- Duplicate collections
- Incorrect balances
- Wrong dates of first delinquency
- Collections that don't belong to you
- Accounts older than seven years

Balance matters far less than accuracy and age. A small, old collection can hurt more than a large, recent one depending on how it's reported.

Section Five: Public Records (Rare but Heavy Impact)

This section may be empty, and that's a good thing.

If it's not, it may include:

- Bankruptcies
- Certain tax liens (where still allowed)

Public records carry significant weight but follow strict reporting rules. Always verify:

- Filing date
- Status (open vs discharged)

- Chapter type for bankruptcy

If a public record is reporting longer than legally allowed, it does not belong on your report. Period.

Section Six: Credit Inquiries (Lower Priority Than You Think)

This section shows who has accessed your credit.

You'll see:

- Hard inquiries (from credit applications)
- Soft inquiries (background checks, pre-approvals)

Hard inquiries matter, but they're often overblown. A few inquiries won't destroy your score.

What to watch for:

- Inquiries you don't recognize
- Multiple inquiries from the same lender on different dates
- Inquiries tied to fraud

If everything looks legitimate, don't lose sleep here.

Section Seven: Consumer Statements and Remarks (Almost Ignored by Lenders)

Sometimes you'll see personal statements or remarks added by you or a creditor.

Here's the honest truth: most lenders ignore these completely.

They don't fix credit. They don't explain away late payments. They mostly just take up space.

Read them once, then move on.

How to Prioritize Like a Professional

If you're overwhelmed, use this order:

- Trade lines
- Payment history
- Collections and charge-offs
- Public records
- Personal information
- Inquiries
- Statements

This priority list alone will save you weeks of wasted effort.

The Big Picture

Your credit report is not a moral judgment. It's a technical document. Once you know which sections matter most, you stop reacting emotionally and start acting strategically.

In the next chapter, we'll shift from reports to scores and break down how all of this data turns into that three-digit number everyone obsesses over. And I promise, it'll make a lot more sense than you think.

Chapter 2: Decoding Your Credit Score

So you finally worked up the courage to check your credit score, and the number that popped up made you question every life choice since high school. Don't panic. Your credit score is basically your financial GPA, except it actually matters after graduation and nobody explained the grading system. Is 680 good? Is 720 great? Why did it drop fifteen points when you paid off a credit card? And why do you have seventeen different scores depending on which app you check? I spent weeks obsessing over these questions, refreshing my score like a teenager checking Instagram likes. Turns out, there's actually logic behind the madness, and once you understand how the scoring models work, you can stop losing sleep over random fluctuations.

This chapter examines the mathematical algorithms and methodologies used to calculate credit scores, with particular focus on FICO and VantageScore models. You will gain insight into the five primary factors that determine your score: payment history, credit utilization, length of credit history, credit mix, and new credit inquiries. We will analyze score ranges and their real-world implications for loan approvals, interest rates, and financial opportunities. Furthermore, this chapter dispels common misconceptions about credit scoring and explains the frequency and circumstances under which your score updates, providing you with realistic expectations for score improvement timelines.

2.1 FICO vs VantageScore: Understanding Different Scoring Models

If you've ever checked your credit score in three different apps and gotten three different numbers, congratulations—you've just met the confusing world of credit scoring models. This is usually the point where people assume the system is rigged, broken, or personally out to get them. After 20 years in this industry, I can confirm: it's not personal, but it is unnecessarily complicated.

The most important thing to understand right away is this: you don't have one credit score. You have many. Dozens, actually. But two scoring models dominate the conversation: FICO and VantageScore. If you understand how these two work and, more importantly, which one actually matters when money is on the line, you'll stop stressing over random numbers and start focusing on what counts.

Why There Are Multiple Credit Scoring Models

Credit scores exist for one reason: to predict risk. Lenders want to know how likely you are to repay a debt on time. Different companies approached this problem in different ways, using different math, assumptions, and priorities.

Think of it like weather apps. They're all using data, but one says there's a 30% chance of rain and another says 50%. Same sky, different models.

The problem isn't that scores differ. The problem is nobody explained this to consumers.

What Is FICO, Really?

FICO stands for Fair Isaac Corporation, the company that created the original credit scoring model back in 1989. FICO is the gold standard. It's the score lenders actually use when approving loans.

Here's the reality:

- About 90% of top lenders use FICO scores
- Mortgages, auto loans, and major credit cards rely heavily on FICO
- When interest rates are set, FICO usually decides your fate

FICO isn't just one score. There are multiple versions:

- FICO 8 (most commonly used for credit cards)
- FICO 9
- FICO 10 and 10T
- Industry-specific versions (auto, mortgage, bankcard)

Each version weighs data slightly differently, but the core principles stay the same.

What Is VantageScore?

VantageScore was created in 2006 by the three major credit bureaus as an alternative to FICO. It was designed to be more consumer-friendly and more accessible, especially for people with limited credit history.

You'll see VantageScore most often in:

- Credit monitoring apps
- Banking apps
- Free credit score websites

VantageScore is not useless, but it is less influential when it comes to actual lending decisions.

Here's where people get tripped up: VantageScore updates quickly and often reacts more dramatically to small changes. That can feel encouraging—or terrifying—depending on the day.

Key Differences Between FICO and VantageScore

Let's break this down in plain English.

1. Lender Usage

- **FICO:** Widely used by lenders
- **VantageScore:** Mostly used for consumer education

If you're applying for real credit, FICO is the score that matters most.

2. Credit History Requirements

- FICO typically requires at least six months of activity
- VantageScore can generate a score with less history

This is why people with thin credit files often see a VantageScore before a FICO score.

3. Score Sensitivity

- FICO is more stable
- VantageScore can swing more dramatically month to month

If your score jumped 40 points overnight, that was probably VantageScore.

4. Treatment of Paid Collections

- Older FICO models may still count paid collections
- Newer models and VantageScore are more forgiving

This difference alone causes a lot of confusion.

Why Your Scores Don't Match Across Apps

Here's the short list of reasons:

- Different scoring models
- Different bureau data
- Different update schedules
- Different versions of the same model

So no, one app isn't "wrong." They're just not showing the same thing.

This is why obsessively refreshing your score across apps is a terrible hobby. Trust me, I've been there.

Which Score Should You Focus On?

Here's my professional answer after two decades in this space:

- **If you're rebuilding credit:** focus on report accuracy and habits, not the number
- **If you're preparing for a loan:** focus on FICO
- **If you're monitoring trends:** VantageScore is fine

Your behavior affects all models over time. The difference is which one lenders actually care about when it's time to say yes or no.

A Common Mistake I See All the Time

People try to "game" one score they see in an app. They make decisions based on that number alone. Then they apply for a loan and get blindsided by a completely different score.

Don't do that.

Use free scores as feedback, not validation.

The Takeaway

FICO is the language lenders speak. VantageScore is a helpful translation, not the final word. When you understand which model matters in which situation, you stop chasing numbers and start making moves that actually improve your financial life.

In the next section, we'll break down the five factors that determine your credit score and show you exactly where to focus your effort for the biggest impact.

2.2 The Five Factors That Determine Your Credit Score

If credit scores had a user manual, it would start with this chapter. Every credit score—FICO, VantageScore, all the fancy versions lenders don't explain—boils down to the same five factors. Different models tweak the math slightly, but the ingredients never change.

The problem isn't that people don't try to improve their credit. The problem is they focus on the wrong things. I've watched people obsess over closing accounts, opening accounts, paying off the "wrong" card, or disputing things that were never hurting them in the first place. That's like rearranging furniture while the house is on fire.

Let's put out the fire first.

Factor #1: Payment History (About 35%)

This is the heavyweight champion of your credit score. Payment history carries more weight than everything else, and it's not even close.

Payment history looks at:

- Whether you pay on time
- How often you're late
- How late you are (30, 60, 90 days)
- How recent the late payments are

One missed payment can hurt. Multiple late payments can haunt you for years. The more recent the late payment, the more damage it does.

Here's something people hate hearing but need to: paying late once is worse than carrying a balance for a few months. The system punishes unreliability more than debt.

Practical advice:

- Set autopay for at least the minimum
- Add calendar reminders as backup
- Treat due dates like deadlines, not suggestions

If you fix nothing else, fix this.

Factor #2: Credit Utilization (About 30%)

Credit utilization is how much of your available credit you're using. This factor alone confuses more people than anything else.

Utilization is calculated by:

- Individual card balances
- Total balances across all cards

If you have a $1,000 limit and a $900 balance, you're using 90%. That looks risky—even if you pay on time every month.

General guidelines:

- Under 30% is good
- Under 10% is excellent
- Over 50% hurts
- Maxed out is brutal

Here's the part nobody explains: when you pay matters. Utilization is usually reported when the statement closes, not when the bill is due.

I've seen people gain 30–40 points just by paying balances down before the statement date.

Factor #3: Length of Credit History (About 15%)

This factor answers one simple question: how long have you been using credit?

It looks at:

- Age of your oldest account
- Age of your newest account
- Average age of all accounts

This is why closing old accounts can backfire. That ancient credit card you never use might be doing more good than harm just by existing.

You can't rush time, but you can avoid hurting yourself:

- Don't close old accounts unless there's a strong reason
- Think carefully before opening multiple new accounts

Length rewards patience and consistency, not activity.

Factor #4: Credit Mix (About 10%)

Credit mix looks at the variety of credit types you have.

Examples include:

- Credit cards (revolving)
- Auto loans (installment)
- Mortgages
- Student loans

This factor is relatively minor, but it can matter when you're trying to move from "good" to "excellent."

Important reality check: never take on debt just to improve credit mix. That's like buying a car to improve your parking skills.

If you already have different types of credit, great. If not, this will improve naturally over time.

Factor #5: New Credit and Inquiries (About 10%)

This factor looks at:

- How many new accounts you've opened
- How recently you applied for credit
- How many hard inquiries appear on your report

Hard inquiries usually cost a few points each and fade over time. Multiple inquiries in a short period can make you look desperate for credit, which lenders don't love.

Practical rule:

- Don't apply for credit unless you have a reason
- Space applications out when possible

This factor is often overblown. It matters, but it's not the villain people make it out to be.

How These Factors Work Together

Here's the big picture most people miss: you don't need perfection in all five areas.

I've seen people with:

- High utilization but perfect payment history

- Short credit history but no late payments
- Limited credit mix but excellent scores

Payment history and utilization do most of the heavy lifting. Everything else fine-tunes the result.

What People Waste Time On

Let me save you some frustration. These things have little to no positive impact:

- Closing paid-off accounts to "clean things up"
- Carrying a balance on purpose
- Paying interest to "build credit"
- Disputing accurate positive accounts

Credit scores reward consistency, not creativity.

The Takeaway

If you remember nothing else from this chapter, remember this:

- Pay on time, every time
- Keep balances low
- Let time do its job

Everything else is strategy, not survival.

In the next section, we'll talk about score ranges and what they actually mean for your financial life—not what the internet forums think they mean.

2.3 Score Ranges and What They Mean for Your Financial Life

At some point, everyone with a credit score asks the same question: "Is this good?" You see a number—643, 702, 781—and immediately try to decode what it says about you as a person. Let me stop you right there. A credit score is not a personality test, a moral judgment, or a prediction of your future success. It's a risk score, and its only job is to answer one boring question for lenders: How likely is this person to pay us back on time?

Still, that number has real-world consequences, so let's translate it into something useful.

The Standard Credit Score Ranges (FICO-Based)

Most lenders use FICO score ranges that look roughly like this:

- **300–579:** Poor
- **580–669:** Fair
- **670–739:** Good
- **740–799:** Very Good
- **800–850:** Excellent

These ranges aren't random. They're thresholds lenders use to decide:

- Whether to approve you
- What interest rate you get
- How much extra risk padding they need

Moving from one range to the next can literally change the cost of your life.

Poor Credit (300–579): Survival Mode

If your score is in this range, you already know it. You don't need a chart. You feel it every time you apply for anything.

What this range usually means:

- High likelihood of denial
- Sky-high interest rates if approved
- Security deposits required
- Limited credit options

Common causes:

- Recent late payments
- Collections or charge-offs
- High utilization
- Short or damaged credit history

Here's the hopeful part: this range is the easiest to escape. Even small improvements—on-time payments, reduced balances, correcting errors—can create noticeable jumps.

This stage isn't permanent. It's a starting point.

Fair Credit (580–669): Expensive Approval

This is the awkward middle ground. You're not locked out, but you're paying for past mistakes.

What to expect:

- Approvals with conditions
- Higher interest rates

- Lower credit limits
- Limited lender options

This is where lenders say "yes... but."

A move from 620 to 680 might not feel dramatic, but it can:

- Cut interest rates
- Reduce required deposits
- Open better credit products

Most people don't realize how close they are to "good" credit from here.

Good Credit (670–739): The Sweet Spot

This range is where life gets easier.

What changes here:

- Consistent approvals
- Reasonable interest rates
- Better credit card offers
- More negotiating power

Here's a secret lenders won't advertise: most people with good credit get approved just as often as people with excellent credit. The biggest difference is pricing, not access.

If you're in this range, you've already done a lot right. Now it's about optimization, not repair.

Very Good Credit (740–799): Prime Territory

This is where lenders start competing for you.

Expect:

- Low interest rates
- Higher credit limits
- Premium card offers
- Easier approvals for large loans

This range offers diminishing returns. The jump from 750 to 790 feels good, but it won't change your life the way moving from 620 to 680 does.

Still, this is a great place to be. Enjoy it.

Excellent Credit (800–850): Bragging Rights (Mostly)

Let's be honest: an 820 score is impressive. But from a practical standpoint, the difference between 780 and 820 is mostly emotional.

What excellent credit gets you:

- Best advertised rates
- Maximum flexibility
- Instant approvals in many cases

What it doesn't do:

- Make loans free
- Guarantee approval regardless of income
- Protect you from bad decisions

I've seen people with 820 scores get denied because of debt-to-income ratios. Credit is powerful, but it's not magic.

Why Lenders Care About Ranges, Not Points

Lenders don't obsess over single points the way consumers do. They look at risk buckets. Crossing a threshold matters more than inching within one.

Example:

- **669 vs 670:** Big difference
- **720 vs 725:** Not much difference

This is why chasing perfection can be a waste of energy.

How Score Ranges Affect Real-Life Costs

Your score impacts:

- Mortgage interest rates
- Auto loan pricing
- Insurance premiums (in many states)
- Utility deposits
- Rental approvals
- Even some job screenings

Over time, a lower score can cost tens of thousands of dollars. Not because lenders hate you—but because risk costs money.

The Mindset Shift That Changes Everything

- Stop asking, "How high can my score go?"
- Start asking, "What range do I need for my next goal?"
- Buying a house?
- Refinancing a car?
- Applying for premium cards?

Each goal has a practical score threshold. Hit that, and stop stressing.

The Takeaway

Credit score ranges are signposts, not finish lines. Moving up one range can change your financial options far more than perfecting a number within it.

In the next section, we'll talk about how often credit scores update—and why checking them obsessively is one of the fastest ways to lose your sanity.

2.4 How Often Your Credit Score Updates

If checking your credit score were an Olympic sport, some of you would be medal contenders. I get it. When you're trying to improve your credit, that number feels like a heartbeat monitor. You pay a bill, refresh the app. You pay another bill, refresh again. Nothing happens. Panic.

After 20 years in this business, let me reassure you: your credit score is not broken, frozen, or personally mad at you. It just doesn't work the way most people think it does.

Let's clear that up.

The Most Important Thing to Understand First

Your credit score does not update on a fixed schedule.

There is no:

- Weekly refresh
- Monthly reset
- Magic "score update day"

Your score updates only when new information is reported to the credit bureaus and processed. No new data, no new score.

That's it. That's the rule.

What Actually Triggers a Score Update

Your score recalculates when one or more of these things happen:

- A creditor reports a new balance
- A payment is reported (on-time or late)

- A new account is added
- An account is closed
- A collection is added or removed
- A dispute result updates the report
- A hard inquiry is added

Every time your credit report changes, your score can change. Sometimes it does. Sometimes it doesn't. Both are normal.

How Often Do Creditors Report Information?

Most creditors report once per month, but here's the catch: they all report on different days.

Common reporting times:

- On your statement closing date
- At the end of the billing cycle
- At the end of the calendar month

This means:

- Paying today might not show for weeks
- Paying after the statement closes may not affect utilization until next cycle
- This is why timing matters, especially with credit cards.

Why Paying a Bill Doesn't Always Change Your Score

This is where people get frustrated.

You pay your credit card in full. You feel responsible. You expect a reward. Then... nothing.

Here's why:

- On-time payments often just maintain your score
- The system expects you to pay on time
- Improvements usually come from reducing risk, not meeting expectations

Think of it like work. Showing up on time doesn't get you a raise. It just keeps you employed.

Why Scores Sometimes Drop "For No Reason"

This is one of the most common complaints I hear.

Possible reasons:

- A balance increased slightly
- A card reported higher utilization
- An old account aged off and changed averages
- A hard inquiry posted
- A lender updated information later than expected

Most small drops are temporary. Overreacting is how people make bad credit decisions.

Credit Monitoring Apps vs Reality

Apps update scores:

- Daily
- Weekly

- On their own schedule

That does not mean your actual score changed that often. It just means the app refreshed its display.

Also important: many apps show VantageScore, which is more sensitive and changes more dramatically than FICO.

Use apps to watch trends, not to diagnose your self-worth.

How Long Real Improvements Take

Here's a realistic timeline based on experience:

- **Utilization changes:** 30–45 days
- **On-time payment impact:** long-term, cumulative
- **Removal of negative items:** 30–90 days after correction
- **Recovery from late payments:** months to years

If someone promises instant permanent score increases, they're selling something.

How Often Should You Check Your Score?

- Professionally?
- Once a month is plenty during rebuilding
- Once every few months when stable

Checking more often does not make it improve faster. It just raises your blood pressure.

The Healthy Way to Track Progress

Instead of asking:

- *"Why didn't my score go up today?"*

Ask:

- *"Did my report change this month?"*
- *"Did my balances go down?"*
- *"Did I avoid late payments?"*

Those are the actions that move scores.

The Takeaway

Your credit score updates when your credit report updates. Not before. Not on demand. Not because you're anxious.

Focus on actions, not refresh buttons. In the next section, we'll debunk the most common credit score myths that keep people stuck and stressed.

2.5 Common Myths About Credit Scores Debunked

If I had a dollar for every credit myth I've heard over the last 20 years, I'd have an 850 score and a beach house. Credit misinformation spreads faster than the truth because it sounds logical, gets repeated online, and usually comes from someone who "heard it from a guy who works at a bank."

Let's clean this up.

These myths don't just confuse people—they actively keep them stuck. I'm going to walk through the biggest ones, explain why they're wrong, and tell you what actually matters instead.

Myth #1: Checking Your Credit Score Lowers It

This one refuses to die.

Truth: Checking your own credit score does not lower it. Ever.

When you check your score or report yourself, it's a soft inquiry, and soft inquiries do not affect your credit. Period.

What does affect your score is when a lender checks your credit after you apply for something. That's a hard inquiry.

If checking your score lowered it, I would've destroyed my credit decades ago just doing my job.

Myth #2: Carrying a Balance Helps Your Score

This myth has probably cost people millions in unnecessary interest.

Truth: You do not need to carry a balance to build credit.

Credit scores reward:

- On-time payments
- Low utilization
- They do not reward paying interest.

You can pay your balance in full every month and still have excellent credit. Anyone telling you otherwise either doesn't understand credit or works for a credit card company.

Myth #3: Closing Credit Cards Improves Your Score

This sounds logical. Less credit, less risk, right?

Wrong.

Truth: Closing accounts often hurts your score by:

- Reducing available credit
- Increasing utilization
- Shortening credit history

Unless a card has an annual fee you can't justify or creates a spending problem, closing it is usually unnecessary.

Old, boring cards are often your best friends.

Myth #4: You Should Dispute Everything Negative

I see this one destroy otherwise decent credit reports.

Truth: Disputing accurate information does not help and can backfire.

Credit repair is not about volume. It's about accuracy. Disputing legitimate accounts can:

- Waste time
- Trigger re-verification

- Delay real progress

You dispute errors, not regrets.

Myth #5: Paid Collections Don't Hurt Your Score

This one hurts because it feels so unfair.

Truth: Paid collections can still impact your score, depending on the scoring model.

Paying a collection does not automatically remove it. That's why strategy matters. Sometimes negotiation is better than rushing to pay.

The goal is deletion, not just payment.

Myth #6: Income Affects Your Credit Score

People with high incomes are always shocked by this.

Truth: Your income is not part of your credit score.

You can make $30,000 or $300,000 and have the same score. Income matters to lenders, but not to scoring models.

Credit scores measure behavior, not wealth.

Myth #7: You Only Have One Credit Score

We covered this earlier, but it's worth repeating.

Truth: You have multiple credit scores across different models and bureaus.

The number you see in an app is a reference point, not a universal truth.

Myth #8: Once Your Credit Is Bad, It's Always Bad

This myth keeps people from even trying.

Truth: Credit is dynamic. It changes constantly.

Late payments fade. Errors get corrected. New positive history adds weight. I've seen people go from the low 500s to the 700s in under two years—legitimately.

Your past does not permanently define your score.

Myth #9: Credit Repair Is Illegal or a Scam

This one comes from misunderstanding.

Truth: Credit repair is legal when it focuses on correcting inaccurate or unverifiable information.

What's illegal:

- Lying
- Creating fake identities
- Credit "washing" schemes

Knowing your rights and using them is not a scam. It's consumer protection.

Myth #10: You Need Perfect Credit to Win

Let me end with a big one.

Truth: You don't need perfect credit. You need appropriate credit.

Most financial goals have a threshold, not a perfection requirement. Once you hit that range, further obsessing has diminishing returns.

The Real Truth About Credit Scores

Credit scores are predictable, not mysterious. They respond to behavior, not emotion. When you understand what matters and ignore the noise, progress becomes a lot easier—and a lot less stressful.

In the next chapter, we'll shift gears and start identifying errors and inaccuracies that may be dragging your score down for reasons that have nothing to do with your behavior at all.

Chapter 3: Identifying Errors and Inaccuracies

Plot twist: your terrible credit score might not even be your fault. I discovered this delightful fact when I found three accounts on my credit report that belonged to someone with a similar name who apparently loved maxing out credit cards. Thanks, Steven with a V instead of my Stephen with a PH. Credit report errors are shockingly common - studies show one in five people have mistakes on their reports. That's not a typo. Twenty percent. These aren't little "oops we spelled your street name wrong" errors either. We're talking phantom debts, payments marked late that you paid on time, and my personal favorite, accounts you closed years ago still showing as open. It's like the credit bureaus hired that one kid from high school who never paid attention in class to manage our financial futures.

This chapter teaches systematic methods for conducting thorough credit report audits to identify inaccuracies, errors, and fraudulent information. You will learn to recognize the most prevalent types of credit reporting mistakes, including incorrect personal information, inaccurate account statuses, erroneous late payment notations, duplicate accounts, and outdated negative items that should have been removed. We will cover techniques for detecting identity theft and fraudulent accounts opened in your name. Additionally, this chapter provides guidance on proper documentation procedures, teaching you to create detailed records of discrepancies that will support your dispute efforts and serve as evidence if escalation becomes necessary.

3.1 Most Common Types of Credit Report Errors

If you've ever looked at your credit report and thought, "There's no way this is all correct," congratulations—you have excellent instincts. After 20 years in this field, I can tell you with confidence that credit report errors are not rare, unusual, or limited to "careless people." They're common, boring, and often expensive.

The credit reporting system runs on massive volumes of data moving automatically between lenders, collectors, and bureaus. When humans barely touch the process, mistakes slip through. A lot. Your job isn't to be offended by that—it's to recognize errors quickly and deal with them strategically.

Let's walk through the most common types of errors I see every single week.

Error #1: Incorrect Personal Information

This one looks harmless, but it's responsible for more problems than people realize.

Common examples:

- Misspelled names
- Wrong middle initial
- Incorrect Social Security number digits
- Addresses you've never lived at
- Employers you never worked for

Why this matters: incorrect personal information can cause your file to be mixed with someone else's. That's how strangers' debts end up on your report.

Minor variations happen. Completely unfamiliar information should be flagged immediately.

Error #2: Accounts That Don't Belong to You

This is the scariest category and, unfortunately, a common one.

You may see:

- Credit cards you never opened
- Loans you never applied for
- Collections you've never heard of

Causes include:

- Identity theft
- Mixed files (similar names or SSNs)
- Clerical errors

If an account isn't yours, it should not be on your report. Period. This is not a "wait and see" situation.

Error #3: Incorrect Account Status

I see this constantly.

Examples:

- Accounts marked "open" that were closed years ago
- Paid accounts still showing balances
- Accounts listed as delinquent when they're current
- Closed accounts still reporting monthly late payments

Status errors make lenders think you're riskier than you actually are. They're also among the easiest errors to document and dispute.

Error #4: Wrong Payment History

This is where scores take the biggest hit.

Common issues:

- Payments marked late that were paid on time
- Payments reported late during deferment or forbearance
- Random late months that don't match statements
- Accounts showing late payments after being closed

One incorrect 30-day late payment can drop a score dramatically. Multiple misreported lates compound the damage.

Never assume a late payment is accurate just because it's old.

Error #5: Duplicate Accounts or Entries

This one is sneaky.

You might see:

- The same debt listed twice
- An original account and a collection both reporting balances
- Multiple collections for the same debt

While some duplication is allowed depending on ownership, double-counting balances or delinquencies is not.

If the same debt appears more than once, it deserves scrutiny.

Error #6: Incorrect Balances or Credit Limits

This affects utilization, which affects your score quickly.

Examples:

- Balance higher than reality
- Credit limit missing or reported as zero
- Old balance still reporting after payment

A missing credit limit can make utilization look maxed out even when it's not. This error alone can suppress your score for months.

Error #7: Re-Aged or Outdated Negative Accounts

This is a big one and often illegal.

Negative items generally fall off after about seven years from the Date of First Delinquency. Some errors include:

- Accounts reporting newer delinquency dates
- Old debts appearing "new" again
- Collections resetting the clock improperly

If the date is wrong, the account may be staying on your report longer than allowed.

Error #8: Incorrect Account Ownership

Especially common with collections.

You might see:

- A collection agency reporting as the original creditor
- An account marked "purchased" when it was only assigned
- Multiple agencies claiming ownership

Ownership affects who you dispute with and how. Incorrect ownership is a legitimate dispute point.

Error #9: Unauthorized Hard Inquiries

Hard inquiries should only appear if you applied for credit.

Watch for:

- Lenders you don't recognize
- Multiple inquiries from the same lender on different dates
- Inquiries tied to fraudulent activity

While inquiries have less impact than other errors, unauthorized ones still matter.

Error #10: Accounts That Should Have Fallen Off

Sometimes, accounts just overstay their welcome.

These include:

- Old collections past reporting limits
- Charge-offs older than allowed
- Bankruptcies reporting beyond legal timeframes

If it's too old to be there, it doesn't belong on your report.

The Pattern Behind Most Errors

Here's the important takeaway: most errors are mechanical, not malicious. Data gets misreported, misapplied, or never updated. That's why proper documentation and calm, precise disputes work better than emotional reactions.

You don't need to fight everything. You need to identify what's wrong.

In the next section, we'll focus specifically on spotting identity theft and fraudulent accounts so you know when an error is just a mistake—and when it's something more serious that needs immediate action.

3.2 Spotting Identity Theft and Fraudulent Accounts

Let me start with some reassurance: seeing something unfamiliar on your credit report does not automatically mean your identity has been stolen. I've watched people spiral because they didn't recognize a lender name that turned out to be a store-branded card or a bank that got acquired three times. That said, actual identity theft is real, it's common, and the faster you spot it, the less damage it does.

After 20 years in this space, I've learned the difference between a simple reporting error and a true fraud situation. Your job isn't to panic—it's to recognize the warning signs and respond correctly.

Let's break it down.

What Identity Theft Looks Like on a Credit Report

Fraud usually shows up in patterns, not isolated typos.

Common red flags include:

- Accounts you never opened
- Hard inquiries you didn't authorize
- Sudden drops in your score with no explanation
- Collection accounts from unfamiliar creditors
- Addresses or phone numbers you've never used

One unfamiliar item might be a mistake. Multiple unfamiliar items appearing around the same time deserve immediate attention.

Fraudulent Accounts vs Reporting Errors

This distinction matters.

Likely reporting error:

- Incorrect balance on a known account
- Wrong account status
- Old address you forgot about
- Creditor name you don't recognize but account details match

Likely fraud:

- Brand-new accounts you never opened
- Inquiries from lenders you never contacted
- Accounts opened in cities or states you've never lived in
- Multiple accounts added within a short period

When fraud is involved, time is not your friend.

The Most Common Types of Credit Fraud

Here's what I see most often:

1. New Account Fraud

- Someone opens a credit card, loan, or phone account using your information.

2. Account Takeover

- A fraudster gains access to an existing account, changes contact info, and runs up charges.

3. Synthetic Identity Fraud

- Your information is combined with someone else's to create a new identity. This one is harder to spot but often shows odd name or address combinations.

4. Collection-Based Fraud

- You only find out about fraud when a collection appears for a debt you never knew existed.

How to Confirm Whether an Account Is Fraudulent

Before taking action, verify:

- Do you recognize the lender under a different name?
- Does the account opening date align with anything in your history?
- Does the address listed match anywhere you've lived?

If the answer is no across the board, treat it as fraud.

Do not call the creditor and "ask questions" casually. That can sometimes make things worse.

Immediate Steps If You Spot Fraud

If you confirm or strongly suspect identity theft, here's what to do—in order:

1. Place a Fraud Alert or Credit Freeze

- A fraud alert warns lenders to verify identity before approving credit. A credit freeze blocks new accounts entirely.

A freeze is free and does not affect your score.

2. Document Everything

Write down:

- Account names
- Account numbers
- Dates opened
- Bureaus reporting the account

Organization matters later.

3. File an Identity Theft Report

- Create an identity theft report with the FTC. This generates documentation you'll need to force removals.

4. Dispute Fraudulent Accounts Properly

- Fraud disputes are different from standard disputes. They require clear identification and supporting documentation.

We'll cover dispute methods in detail in Chapter 4.

Why You Shouldn't Ignore "Small" Fraud

People sometimes ignore:

- Small balances
- Store cards
- Utility accounts

That's a mistake. Fraud rarely stops on its own. Today it's a $300 card. Tomorrow it's a car loan.

Early action limits long-term damage.

How Fraud Affects Your Credit Differently

Fraud-related negative items can often be removed faster than legitimate disputes—if handled correctly. The law provides stronger protections for identity theft victims than for regular reporting errors.

But only if you use the process properly.

What Not to Do

Please avoid these common mistakes:

- Don't pay fraudulent accounts "just to make them go away"
- Don't ignore hard inquiries you don't recognize
- Don't wait months hoping it resolves itself
- Don't dispute fraud as "not mine" without documentation

Fraud requires a paper trail.

The Long-Term Protection Mindset

Once you've dealt with fraud, prevention matters:

- Monitor your reports regularly
- Keep freezes in place unless applying for credit
- Shred sensitive documents
- Be cautious with online forms and phone calls

Identity theft is frustrating, but it's manageable when caught early.

The Takeaway

Errors are annoying. Fraud is urgent. Knowing the difference saves time, money, and stress. If something on your report truly doesn't belong to you, trust that instinct and act quickly—but strategically.

Next, we'll talk about recognizing outdated or obsolete information that should no longer be on your credit report at all, even if it was once accurate.

3.3 Recognizing Outdated or Obsolete Information

One of the most frustrating things about credit reports is this: just because something was accurate once doesn't mean it's allowed to stay forever. Credit reporting has time limits. Hard ones. And yet, I regularly see negative accounts hanging around like an ex who refuses to move out even though the lease ended years ago.

After 20 years of reviewing credit reports, I can tell you that outdated information is one of the most overlooked—and most fixable—problems people have. Not because it's rare, but because people don't know what dates actually matter.

Let's fix that.

The Most Important Date You've Never Paid Attention To

When it comes to negative items, the most powerful date on your credit report is the Date of First Delinquency (often abbreviated as DOFD).

This date marks:

- The first missed payment
- After which the account was never brought current again

Everything else flows from this date.

Most negative items must be removed about seven years from the DOFD—not from when the account was charged off, sold, or paid. If that date is wrong, the account can illegally stay on your report longer than allowed.

This is where a lot of "zombie" accounts come from.

What "Outdated" Actually Means in Credit Reporting

Outdated does not mean:

- Old
- Paid
- Inactive
- Annoying

Outdated means legally past the reporting period.

If an item is still within the allowed timeframe, it can legally remain—even if you hate looking at it.

If it's past the timeframe, it does not belong there. End of story.

Standard Reporting Time Limits (General Rules)

Here are the most common timelines you'll see:

- **Late payments**: 7 years from DOFD
- **Collections:** 7 years from DOFD of the original account
- **Charge-offs**: 7 years from DOFD
- **Repossessions:** 7 years
- **Foreclosures:** 7 years
- **Chapter 7 bankruptcy:** 10 years from filing date
- **Chapter 13 bankruptcy:** 7 years from filing date

If something is showing beyond these limits, it's obsolete.

Common Ways Accounts Get Re-Aged Incorrectly

Re-aging is when a negative account's clock is improperly reset.

This often happens when:

- A collection agency buys an old debt
- A debt is transferred to another collector
- A payment is made years later
- A balance is updated without proper context

Important truth: paying an old debt does not reset the reporting clock. The clock is tied to the original delinquency, not activity afterward.

If you see a collection with a "recent" delinquency date for a debt from years ago, that's a red flag.

How to Spot Obsolete Information on Your Report

When reviewing a negative account, look for:

- Date of first delinquency
- Date opened vs age of account
- Date reported
- Last activity date

Then ask:

- Does this timeline make sense?
- Is this account older than seven years from the first missed payment?
- Does the delinquency date suddenly jump forward?

If dates don't line up logically, investigate further.

Why Obsolete Accounts Hurt More Than They Should

Outdated accounts don't just hurt your score—they create false risk signals. Lenders assume recent problems are more dangerous than old ones. When old negatives linger, they make you look less stable than you actually are.

Removing obsolete information can result in significant score improvement, especially if the item appears recent.

A Common Mistake That Keeps Old Accounts Alive

I see this mistake constantly: people dispute an old account incorrectly, and it comes back updated instead of removed.

When dealing with obsolete information:

- You dispute the age, not the debt
- You reference reporting time limits
- You do not argue about balance or ownership

Precision matters.

What to Document for Obsolete Accounts

Before disputing, gather:

- Evidence of original delinquency date
- Old statements or records if available
- Clear notes comparing dates across bureaus

You don't need a novel. You need clarity.

Why Bureaus Don't Automatically Remove Old Accounts

In theory, they should. In practice, automated systems rely on data provided by furnishers. If the date is wrong, the system doesn't question it unless forced to.

That's where you come in.

The Takeaway

Negative credit information has an expiration date. If it's expired, it doesn't belong on your report—no matter how accurate it once was. Knowing how to spot outdated or re-aged accounts gives you leverage many people never use.

Next, we'll focus on finding duplicate accounts and entries—another common reporting issue that quietly drags scores down without people realizing why.

3.4 Finding Duplicate Accounts and Entries

Duplicate accounts are one of the sneakiest credit report problems out there. They don't jump off the page screaming, "Hey, this is wrong!" Instead, they quietly double the damage while looking technically legitimate—unless you know exactly what to look for.

After 20 years in this field, I can tell you this: a single debt should only hurt you once. If the same obligation is being counted multiple times, something is wrong, and it deserves your attention.

Let's break down how duplicates happen, how to spot them, and how to tell the difference between what's allowed and what isn't.

What Counts as a Duplicate Entry?

A duplicate occurs when the same debt appears more than once in a way that exaggerates its impact.

Common examples:

- The same collection listed twice by the same agency
- Multiple collection agencies reporting balances for the same debt
- An original account and a collection both showing past-due balances incorrectly
- The same account listed under slightly different creditor names

Not every "repeat-looking" entry is an error, but many are.

Why Duplicate Accounts Happen So Often

Most duplicates happen during debt transfers.

Here's the usual chain of events:

- You fall behind on a bill
- The creditor charges it off
- The debt is sold or assigned to a collector
- Another collector later gets involved

Each handoff increases the chance of bad reporting.

Sometimes old collectors forget to stop reporting. Sometimes new collectors start reporting incorrectly. Sometimes both happen at once.

What Is Allowed (This Part Matters)

Here's what can legally appear on your report:

- An original creditor showing a charge-off with a zero balance
- A collection agency reporting the same debt separately
- Multiple collection agencies listed if ownership changes over time (with conditions)

Key rule: only one active balance should be reporting at a time.

If more than one company claims you owe money for the same debt, that's a problem.

What Is Not Allowed

These are legitimate duplicate errors:

- Two collections reporting balances for the same debt at the same time
- A collection and original creditor both showing past-due balances

- Same debt appearing twice under the same collector
- Re-aged duplicates with different delinquency dates
- Closed accounts continuing to report as open duplicates

If it looks like you owe the same dollar twice, it's wrong.

How to Spot Duplicates Like a Pro

When reviewing your report, line up entries and compare:

- Original creditor name
- Account number (even partial matches matter)
- Balance amounts
- Dates of first delinquency
- Account opening dates

Ask yourself:

- Are these entries tied to the same original debt?
- Are balances being counted more than once?
- Do dates line up suspiciously well?

Duplicates often reveal themselves through matching balances or identical delinquency timelines.

The Collection-on-Collection Red Flag

This one deserves special attention.

If you see:

- Collection Agency A reporting a balance

- Collection Agency B reporting a balance
- Same original creditor
- Same amount or similar dates

That's usually not allowed. Only the current owner or assigned collector should be reporting a balance.

Older agencies should show zero balance or be removed entirely.

Why Duplicate Entries Hurt More Than You Think

Duplicate accounts:

- Inflate utilization
- Multiply negative payment history
- Make your report look chaotic
- Lower approval odds even if your score survives

Lenders don't always analyze deeply. They see multiple negatives and move on.

How People Accidentally Make Duplicates Worse

A common mistake: paying the wrong party.

If you pay a collection agency that no longer owns the debt, the active collector may still report the balance. Now you've paid money and still have damage.

Ownership matters.

What to Document When You Find a Duplicate

Before disputing, write down:

Which entries appear to be duplicates

- Matching balances or dates
- Which company currently claims ownership
- Which entries should show zero balance or be removed

Clear documentation makes disputes easier and faster.

The Takeaway

Duplicate accounts aren't just annoying—they distort your credit profile. Once you know how to spot them, they're hard to miss. A debt should only tell its story once, not on repeat.

In the next section, we'll talk about documenting errors properly so your disputes don't get ignored, dismissed, or delayed.

3.5 Documenting Errors for Dispute Preparation

This is the part nobody wants to do, and it's the part that separates people who try to fix their credit from people who actually succeed.

You can spot every error on your credit report and still get nowhere if you don't document them properly. Credit bureaus don't respond to frustration, fairness arguments, or "this doesn't seem right." They respond to clear, organized, verifiable documentation.

After 20 years of doing this, I can tell you: most disputes fail not because the consumer is wrong, but because the consumer is sloppy.

Let's make sure that's not you.

Why Documentation Is Everything

Credit disputes are legal processes, not customer service conversations.

When you dispute an item, the bureau:

- Forwards your dispute to the furnisher
- Requests verification
- Updates the report based on the response

If your dispute is vague, emotional, or unsupported, it's easy to dismiss. If it's precise and documented, it forces real review.

Think of this like court, not therapy.

What You Should Document for Every Error

For each disputed item, you need a mini case file.

At minimum, document:

- Credit bureau reporting the error
- Creditor or collection agency name
- Account number (partial is fine)
- Type of error (late payment, balance, ownership, date)
- Why it's incorrect
- What correction you're requesting

This information should be consistent across all disputes.

Supporting Documents That Actually Help

Not all documents are created equal.

Strong documentation includes:

- Payment confirmations
- Bank statements
- Account statements
- Settlement letters
- Identity theft reports (for fraud)
- Correspondence from creditors
- Old credit reports showing correct information

Weak documentation:

- Screenshots from apps
- Personal explanations without proof

- Highlighted reports with no context

If a document doesn't prove something factual, it won't carry much weight.

How to Organize Your Dispute Files

You don't need fancy software. You need structure.

My recommended system:

- One folder per bureau
- One subfolder per disputed account
- Clear file names with dates

Example:

- Experian / CapitalOne_LatePayment_2019 / BankStatement_Mar2019.pdf
- This saves you time when disputes escalate.
- Writing Notes That Strengthen Disputes

Before you ever send a dispute, write a short, factual summary:

- What is wrong
- Why it's wrong
- What should happen

No emotion. No backstory. No insults.

Credit bureaus are not impressed by passion. They are impressed by clarity.

Common Documentation Mistakes to Avoid

Please avoid these:

- Disputing multiple errors in one vague explanation
- Sending unnecessary documents
- Highlighting entire statements without explanation
- Submitting different explanations to different bureaus
- Forgetting to keep copies

Always assume you'll need your records again.

When Documentation Is Mandatory

Some disputes require extra care:

- Identity theft
- Fraudulent accounts
- Re-aged accounts
- Obsolete information
- Ownership disputes

In these cases, documentation isn't optional—it's required.

Why Precision Beats Volume

More disputes does not mean better results. Sending ten weak disputes often fails where two strong ones succeed.

Accuracy forces accountability.

The Takeaway

Documenting errors is not exciting, but it's powerful. When you approach disputes like a professional—organized, factual, and prepared—you stop getting form-letter responses and start seeing real corrections.

In the next chapter, we'll break down the dispute process step by step and show you exactly how to turn your documentation into results.

Chapter 4: The Dispute Process Explained

Alright, detective, you've found the errors. Now what? I'll never forget my first dispute letter - I wrote this passionate three-page essay about injustice and fairness, basically treating Experian like they were my therapist. Guess what? They didn't care. They sent back a form letter that basically said "thanks for playing." That's when I learned that disputing credit report errors isn't about emotions or fairness. It's about following a specific legal process that forces these bureaus to actually investigate your claims within thirty days. The Fair Credit Reporting Act is basically your superhero cape in this fight, and once you know how to use it, those credit bureaus have to take you seriously. No tears. No begging. Just legal obligations they can't ignore.

This chapter provides detailed instruction on the formal dispute process as governed by the Fair Credit Reporting Act. You will learn to craft effective dispute letters that include all necessary information while avoiding common mistakes that lead to automatic denials. We will examine the documentation requirements for supporting your claims and explain the credit bureau's legal obligation to investigate disputes within thirty days. This chapter outlines what constitutes a reasonable investigation, how to interpret dispute results, and the specific steps to take when bureaus dismiss your disputes or fail to correct verified errors. Understanding this process is essential for successfully removing inaccurate information from your credit reports.

4.1 Your Rights Under the Fair Credit Reporting Act

This is the chapter where things stop feeling unfair and start feeling manageable.

For years, I thought credit bureaus had all the power and consumers just had to live with whatever showed up on their reports. Turns out, that's completely wrong. The reason disputes work at all is because of one very important law: the Fair Credit Reporting Act, or FCRA.

You don't need to be a lawyer to use it. You just need to understand what it actually gives you the right to do—and what it forces credit bureaus and creditors to do whether they like it or not.

What the FCRA Is (In Plain English)

The Fair Credit Reporting Act is a federal law designed to make sure:

- Credit information is accurate
- Credit information is fair
- Credit information is verifiable

The law exists because Congress recognized something important: consumers cannot function financially if private companies are allowed to report incorrect data with no accountability.

This law doesn't make credit bureaus nice. It makes them legally obligated.

Your Core Rights Under the FCRA

Let's break this down into practical rights you can actually use.

Right #1: You Have the Right to Accurate Information

This sounds obvious, but it's the foundation of everything.

Credit bureaus and data furnishers are required to:

- Report information accurately
- Correct or remove inaccurate data
- Not report information they cannot verify

If information is wrong, misleading, incomplete, or unverifiable, it does not belong on your report.

Accuracy is not optional.

Right #2: You Have the Right to Dispute Errors

If you find inaccurate information, you have the legal right to dispute it—for free.

Once you dispute:

- The credit bureau must investigate
- The furnisher must verify the information
- The burden of proof is on them, not you

You do not have to prove you're innocent. They have to prove they're right.

This is one of the most misunderstood parts of the process.

Right #3: The 30-Day Investigation Rule

This is where the law has teeth.

After receiving your dispute, the credit bureau generally has 30 days to:

- Conduct a reasonable investigation
- Contact the furnisher

- Review the response
- Update or remove the information

If they can't verify the item within that time frame, it must be removed or corrected.

No extensions just because they're busy.

Right #4: The Right to See the Results

After the investigation, you have the right to:

- Receive written results
- See what changed
- Know if information was verified, corrected, or removed

If something stays on your report, you're entitled to know why.

Silence is not compliance.

Right #5: The Right to Dispute Directly With the Furnisher

You are not limited to disputing only with credit bureaus.

You also have the right to dispute directly with:

- Credit card companies
- Loan servicers
- Collection agencies
- Any company reporting data about you

This becomes very important in advanced dispute strategies, which we'll cover later.

Right #6: Protection Against Re-Reporting Errors

If an item is removed due to a dispute, it cannot simply be added back later without:

- Proper verification
- Notification to you

This prevents the same error from popping back up quietly.

When re-reporting rules are violated, you have leverage.

Right #7: The Right to Free Credit Reports

You are entitled to:

- Free credit reports as allowed by law
- Additional free reports after adverse actions (like denials)
- Free reports if you're a victim of identity theft

You never have to pay just to see what's being reported about you.

Right #8: Special Rights for Identity Theft Victims

If you're a victim of identity theft, the FCRA gives you stronger protections:

- Faster removal of fraudulent accounts
- Ability to block fraudulent information
- Additional documentation rights

Fraud disputes are not treated the same as regular errors—and that works in your favor.

What the FCRA Does Not Do

Let's be clear about limits so expectations stay realistic.

The FCRA does not:

- Remove accurate negative information just because it's inconvenient
- Instantly fix credit overnight
- Prevent lenders from reporting legitimate late payments
- Guarantee approval for credit

It enforces accuracy, not forgiveness.

Why Knowing Your Rights Changes the Dynamic

Once you understand the FCRA, disputes stop feeling like requests and start feeling like legal notices. You're no longer asking for a favor. You're invoking a right.

That mindset shift is everything.

Credit bureaus don't respond to anger. They respond to obligations.

The Takeaway

The Fair Credit Reporting Act is your foundation. Every successful dispute, correction, and removal rests on it. When you know your rights, you stop feeling powerless and start acting strategically.

In the next section, we'll get practical and break down how to write effective dispute letters that actually trigger these legal obligations instead of getting ignored.

4.2 Writing Effective Dispute Letters to Credit Bureaus

This is where most people go wrong.

They sit down to write a dispute letter like they're auditioning for a courtroom drama—three emotional pages about how unfair life has been, how they're a good person, and how the credit bureau is ruining everything. I've written those letters before. They feel great. They also don't work.

Credit bureaus don't respond to feelings. They respond to structure, clarity, and legal obligation. After 20 years of doing this, I can tell you with certainty: a short, boring, precise dispute letter beats a passionate essay every single time.

Let me show you how to write letters that actually get results.

First: What a Dispute Letter Is (and Isn't)

A dispute letter is not:

- A negotiation
- A complaint
- A confession
- A life story

A dispute letter is:

- A formal notice
- A request for verification
- A demand for correction if verification fails

You are triggering a legal process under the Fair Credit Reporting Act. Nothing more, nothing less.

The Golden Rules of Effective Dispute Letters

Before we get into structure, follow these rules religiously:

- One account per letter (when possible)
- One error per account
- No emotion
- No unnecessary details
- No admissions of guilt
- Always request investigation

If your letter sounds like customer service feedback, rewrite it.

What Every Dispute Letter Must Include

At minimum, your letter needs:

- Your full name
- Current address
- Date of birth
- Partial Social Security number (last 4 digits)
- The credit bureau you're writing to
- The creditor or collection agency name
- Account number (partial is fine)
- Clear description of the error
- Clear request for correction or removal

Anything missing gives them an excuse to delay.

The Structure That Works (Every Time)

Here's the structure I've used for years with consistent results:

- **Identification** – Who you are
- **Statement of dispute** – What you're disputing
- **Explanation** – Why it's inaccurate or unverifiable
- **Request** – What action you want taken
- **Documentation reference** – What you've attached

That's it. No fluff.

Sample Dispute Letter (Use This Format)

Here's a clean, professional example you can adapt:

[Your Full Name]

[Your Address]

[City, State, ZIP Code]

[Date of Birth]

[Last 4 Digits of SSN]

[Date]

[Credit Bureau Name]

[Credit Bureau Address]

Re: Credit Report Dispute

To Whom It May Concern,

I am writing to formally dispute the accuracy of information appearing on my credit report.

The account listed below is inaccurate and requires investigation:

Creditor Name: ABC Collection Agency

Account Number: XXXX1234

This account does not belong to me / contains inaccurate payment history / is reporting an incorrect balance. Please conduct a reasonable investigation into this matter as required under the Fair Credit Reporting Act.

If the information cannot be verified, I request that it be corrected or removed from my credit report.

Attached are copies of supporting documents for your review.

Please provide written confirmation of the results of your investigation.

Sincerely,

[Your Full Name]

That's it. Notice what's missing? Drama.

How Specific Should You Be?

Specific enough to point to the problem. Not so specific that you argue the case for them.

Good:

- "Payment reported late for March 2022 despite being paid on time"
- "Balance reported incorrectly as $1,240 instead of $0"
- "Account does not belong to me"

Not good:

- “I always pay my bills”
- “This ruined my life”
- “I was going through a hard time”

Facts only.

Supporting Documents: Less Is More

Attach only what supports your claim.

Examples:

- Proof of payment
- Account statements
- Settlement letters
- Identity theft report (for fraud)

Do not send:

- Entire bank histories
- Screenshots with no explanation
- Documents unrelated to the error

Label documents clearly. Make their job easy.

Mail vs Online Disputes (Important)

You can dispute:

- Online
- By mail

Online disputes are faster, but they:

- Limit how much you can explain
- Often use checkboxes
- Create weaker paper trails
- For simple errors, online is fine.
- For serious disputes, mail is stronger.

If you mail disputes:

- Use certified mail when escalating
- Keep copies of everything
- Track delivery dates

Paper trails matter.

Common Mistakes That Get Disputes Ignored

Avoid these at all costs:

- Disputing multiple accounts in one letter
- Disputing accurate information
- Sending form letters copied word-for-word from the internet
- Disputing the same item repeatedly with no new evidence
- Admitting the debt while disputing accuracy

Precision beats repetition.

Timing Matters More Than You Think

Don't dispute everything at once. Focus on:

- High-impact errors first

- Clear inaccuracies
- Items hurting utilization or payment history

Stagger disputes if necessary. You're building leverage, not flooding the system.

The Mindset Shift That Makes This Work

You are not asking credit bureaus to be kind. You are invoking your rights. When your letters are clear, factual, and professional, they force action.

Boring letters win.

In the next section, we'll talk about gathering the right supporting documentation and how to strengthen disputes so they don't come back with the dreaded "verified as accurate" response.

4.3 Gathering Supporting Documentation

This is the part of credit repair that feels tedious but wins cases. Think of supporting documentation as the difference between saying "I'm right" and proving it in a way the system can't ignore.

After 20 years of doing this, I can tell you something most people don't want to hear: credit bureaus believe paper more than people. If it's documented, it's real. If it's not, it's just a story.

Let's talk about how to gather the right documentation without overcomplicating your life.

Why Documentation Carries So Much Weight

When you dispute an item, the bureau doesn't sit there evaluating your character. They forward your dispute to the furnisher and ask one question: Can you verify this information?

Documentation does two things:

- Forces the furnisher to actually look
- Creates accountability if they don't

The stronger your documentation, the harder it is for them to hit you with "verified as accurate" and move on.

The Three Categories of Supporting Documents

Every dispute falls into one of these buckets.

1. Proof the Account Is Wrong

Use this when the account itself is inaccurate or not yours.

Helpful documents include:

- Identity theft report (for fraud)
- Police report (if applicable)
- Affidavit of fraud
- Proof of address showing you never lived where the account was opened
- Statements showing the account belongs to someone else

If the account is not yours, documentation is non-negotiable.

2. Proof the Information Is Reported Incorrectly

This is the most common category.

Use documents like:

- Bank statements showing payments cleared
- Credit card or loan statements
- Payment confirmation emails
- Settlement or payoff letters
- Account closure confirmations

If a payment is marked late but you paid on time, your bank statement is your best friend.

3. Proof the Information Is Obsolete

Use this when an item should have aged off.

Helpful documentation:

- Old credit reports showing earlier delinquency dates
- Statements from the original creditor

- Records showing the account has exceeded reporting limits

Dates matter more than balances here.

What You Don't Need to Send

Sending too much can hurt you.

Avoid:

- Entire bank histories
- Unrelated financial records
- Screenshots from apps
- Highlighted documents with no explanation

Bureaus do not reward effort. They reward relevance.

How to Prepare Documents the Right Way

Follow these best practices:

- Make clear, readable copies
- Circle or highlight the exact line that proves your point
- Write a short note explaining what the document shows
- Never send originals

Your goal is clarity, not volume.

Label Everything (Seriously)

Unlabeled documents slow down investigations.

Good labels look like:

- *"Proof_of_Payment_March2022"*

- *"Settlement_Letter_ABC_Collections"*
- *"BankStatement_Page2_Payment"*

Think like someone who doesn't care but has to process your file anyway.

Special Documentation for Identity Theft

If fraud is involved, you'll usually need:

- Identity theft report
- Government-issued ID copy
- Proof of address

Fraud disputes get stronger protections—but only if you use the correct paperwork.

When You Don't Have Documentation

This happens more than people admit.

If you don't have proof:

- Don't invent it
- Don't guess
- Don't exaggerate

In these cases, disputes rely on verification failure. If the furnisher can't verify, the item must be removed. That's still a valid approach.

How Long to Keep Your Records

Short answer: longer than you think.

I recommend:

- Keeping dispute records for at least 2–3 years

- Keeping identity theft documentation indefinitely
- Saving digital copies backed up securely

Errors have a bad habit of reappearing.

The Takeaway

Supporting documentation turns disputes from requests into obligations. You don't need a mountain of paperwork—you need the right proof, clearly presented.

In the next section, we'll break down the 30-day investigation period, what actually happens during that time, and how to respond if the clock runs out without real action.

4.4 Understanding the 30-Day Investigation Period

This is where patience meets power.

Once you send a dispute, a clock starts ticking. Not a vague "we'll get back to you" clock—a legal one. The 30-day investigation period is the backbone of the dispute process, and understanding how it actually works will keep you from panicking, overreacting, or accidentally sabotaging your own case.

After 20 years of watching this play out, I can tell you: most people lose leverage during these 30 days simply because they don't know what's happening behind the scenes.

Let's fix that.

When the 30-Day Clock Really Starts

Here's the first thing people get wrong: the 30 days do not start when you drop the letter in the mailbox.

The clock starts when:

The credit bureau receives your dispute

That's why tracking matters. If you dispute online, the timestamp is automatic. If you mail disputes, this is where certified mail becomes useful later on—it proves receipt.

Once received, the bureau generally has 30 days to complete the investigation.

What the Credit Bureau Is Supposed to Do

During the investigation period, the credit bureau must:

- Review your dispute

- Forward the dispute to the data furnisher
- Request verification of the information
- Review the furnisher's response
- Update, correct, or remove the item
- Notify you of the results

This is called a "reasonable investigation" under the Fair Credit Reporting Act. Reasonable does not mean perfect, but it does mean more than pressing a button and moving on.

What the Furnisher Is Supposed to Do

The furnisher (creditor or collection agency) must:

- Review the dispute
- Check their records
- Confirm or correct the information
- Respond within the allowed time frame

If they cannot verify the accuracy of the information, the item must be corrected or removed.

This is where weak data breaks.

The One Thing That Stops the Clock

There is exactly one thing that can pause or reset the investigation period:

You sending additional information mid-investigation.

If you submit new documents during the 30 days, the bureau may restart the clock. This isn't always bad, but you should do it intentionally, not accidentally.

That's why preparation before disputing matters.

Why Some Investigations End Early

Sometimes disputes resolve in:

- 10 days
- 14 days
- Even faster

This usually means:

- The furnisher didn't respond
- The information couldn't be verified quickly
- The error was obvious

Fast results are good results.

Why "Verified as Accurate" Happens So Often

This phrase frustrates everyone.

It usually means:

- The furnisher responded
- The bureau accepted the response
- The item stayed

It does not automatically mean the information is correct. It means the system accepted the verification.

That's why documentation, wording, and escalation matter.

What You Should Be Doing During the 30 Days

Here's the professional approach:

- Do not send follow-up letters immediately
- Do not dispute the same item again
- Do not call the bureau repeatedly
- Do not panic

Instead:

- Track dates
- Organize records
- Prepare next steps in case of denial

Silence during this period is normal.

What Happens at the End of the 30 Days

At the end of the investigation, one of three things happens:

- **Item is removed** – Best outcome
- **Item is corrected** – Still a win
- **Item is verified** – Not the end

You should receive written results explaining what changed.

If you don't receive results, that's a problem—and sometimes leverage.

What If the Bureau Misses the Deadline?

If the bureau fails to complete the investigation within the allowed time:

- The item should be removed or corrected
- Continued reporting may violate the FCRA

Missed deadlines don't happen often, but when they do, they matter.

This is where good recordkeeping pays off.

The Biggest Mistake People Make Here

They assume the first result is final.

It's not.

Initial disputes are step one, not the finish line. Many legitimate corrections happen in follow-up rounds when you escalate properly, add pressure, or dispute directly with the furnisher.

The Takeaway

The 30-day investigation period is not dead time—it's leverage time. Understanding what's happening, what to expect, and what not to do keeps you in control.

In the next section, we'll talk about exactly what to do if your dispute is denied or comes back "verified," and how to push forward without starting over or making things worse.

4.5 What to Do If Your Dispute Is Denied

Few things are more annoying than opening a letter from a credit bureau that basically says, "We investigated and everything is accurate." Especially when you know it's not. I've been there. After 20 years in this field, I can tell you this with certainty: a denied dispute is not a dead end—it's a fork in the road.

Most people quit here. That's exactly why the system works the way it does. Persistence, when done correctly, is what separates results from frustration.

Let's talk about what to do next.

First: Understand What "Denied" Actually Means

When a dispute comes back "verified as accurate," it usually means:

- The furnisher responded
- The bureau accepted that response
- The system closed the investigation

It does not necessarily mean:

- The information is correct
- A real human reviewed your evidence
- You're out of options

It means step one didn't work.

Step One: Review the Results Carefully

Before taking any action, read the results letter closely.

Look for:

- What exactly was verified
- Whether any part of the account changed
- Which bureau(s) denied the dispute
- Whether the wording is vague or specific

Sometimes partial corrections slip through. Sometimes nothing changes. Details matter.

Step Two: Identify Why the Dispute Failed

Ask yourself:

- Was my dispute too vague?
- Did I provide enough documentation?
- Did I dispute the wrong aspect (balance instead of date)?
- Did I dispute with the wrong party?

Most failed disputes aren't wrong—they're misdirected.

Step Three: Escalate, Don't Repeat

Repeating the same dispute with the same wording usually gets ignored.

Better options include:

- Adding new documentation
- Clarifying the specific inaccuracy
- Referencing exact dates or amounts
- Changing the dispute target

Escalation is about pressure, not volume.

Option 1: Dispute Directly With the Furnisher

You are legally allowed to dispute directly with the company reporting the information.

This works well when:

- The bureau keeps siding with the furnisher
- You have strong documentation
- The issue is specific and factual

Direct disputes force furnishers to review their own records, not just respond to bureau prompts.

Option 2: Demand Verification, Not Validation

There's a difference between:

- "This is wrong"
- "Prove this is correct"

Requesting verification shifts the burden back to the furnisher. If they can't produce documentation, they're required to correct or remove the item.

This is especially powerful for older accounts and collections.

Option 3: Use Certified Mail to Create a Paper Trail

If disputes keep getting dismissed, switch to certified mail.

Why this matters:

- It proves receipt
- It shows seriousness

- It creates a legal record

You're no longer just clicking buttons. You're documenting compliance—or lack of it.

Option 4: File a Complaint With the CFPB

When bureaus or furnishers stop playing fair, escalation matters.

A CFPB complaint:

- Forces a response
- Requires explanation
- Creates regulatory pressure

This is not a nuclear option—it's a legitimate consumer protection tool.

Option 5: Add a Consumer Statement (Limited Use)

Consumer statements rarely improve scores, but they can help in very specific cases where:

- An explanation is genuinely necessary
- Manual underwriting is involved

Use sparingly. This is not a fix—it's context.

Option 6: Know When to Move On Strategically

Not every denial is worth endless energy.

If an item is:

- Accurate
- Recent
- Well-documented by the creditor

Your time may be better spent:

- Reducing utilization
- Building positive history
- Letting time work in your favor

Smart credit repair is selective.

The Biggest Mistake After a Denial

People either:

- Give up completely
- Or dispute aggressively without strategy

Both waste time.

Progress comes from informed escalation, not emotional reactions.

The Takeaway

A denied dispute isn't failure—it's feedback. It tells you where the resistance is and how strong it is. With the right next move, many "verified" items eventually get corrected or removed.

In the next chapter, we'll move into advanced dispute strategies—the techniques that separate casual attempts from serious results.

Chapter 5: Advanced Dispute Strategies

So the credit bureau came back with "we investigated and the information is accurate" even though you know for a fact it's wrong. Cool. Cool cool cool. Don't throw your laptop out the window just yet. This is where most people give up, and honestly, that's exactly what these companies are counting on. But you're not most people anymore. You're about to learn the advanced tactics that separate casual credit repair attempts from serious results. We're talking about going directly to the creditors who reported the information, using verification methods that make them prove they have proper documentation, and knowing exactly which government agencies to contact when companies refuse to play fair. This is chess, not checkers, and you're about to learn how the grandmasters play.

This chapter introduces advanced credit dispute methodologies for situations where initial dispute attempts prove unsuccessful. You will learn to bypass credit bureaus by disputing directly with data furnishers and original creditors, often yielding faster results. We will explore the Section 623 method for demanding verification and documentation of reported debts. This chapter covers escalation procedures, including filing complaints with the Consumer Financial Protection Bureau and state attorneys general. You will understand when certified mail becomes necessary for creating legally binding paper trails, and we will discuss circumstances under which legal action or consultation with a consumer rights attorney becomes appropriate for resolving persistent credit reporting violations.

5.1 Disputing Directly with Creditors and Data Furnishers

At some point in credit repair, you realize something important: the credit bureaus are middlemen. They don't create the data—they just pass it along. When disputes stall or keep coming back "verified," the smartest move is often to go straight to the source.

After 20 years in this field, I can tell you this is where many stubborn issues finally break. Not because creditors are nicer than bureaus (they're not), but because the law requires them to take direct disputes seriously.

Let's talk about how and when to dispute directly with creditors and data furnishers—and how to do it without making things worse.

What Is a Data Furnisher?

A data furnisher is any company that reports information about you to the credit bureaus.

This includes:

- Credit card companies
- Banks and loan servicers
- Auto lenders
- Mortgage companies
- Collection agencies

If they put data on your credit report, they are a furnisher and have legal responsibilities under the Fair Credit Reporting Act.

Why Direct Disputes Can Be More Effective

When you dispute through a bureau:

- Your dispute is summarized
- Your explanation may be shortened
- Your documents may not be forwarded fully

When you dispute directly:

- The creditor receives your full letter
- They must review their own records
- They must investigate and respond

Direct disputes remove the "telephone game" effect.

When You Should Dispute Directly

Direct disputes work best when:

- A bureau keeps siding with the furnisher
- The error is specific and documentable
- You're disputing payment history, balances, or dates
- You need the furnisher to prove ownership or accuracy

They're less effective when the issue is purely a bureau formatting error.

Your Legal Right to Dispute Directly

Under the FCRA, you have the right to send a written dispute directly to the furnisher.

Once received, the furnisher must:

- Conduct a reasonable investigation

- Review relevant information
- Report results back to the bureaus
- Correct or delete inaccurate data

Ignoring a valid direct dispute can create serious compliance issues for them.

How to Write a Direct Dispute Letter

The structure is similar to bureau disputes but slightly more direct.

Key elements:

- Clear identification
- Specific account reference
- Exact error being disputed
- Request for verification or correction
- Reference to your rights under the FCRA

No threats. No emotion. Just clarity.

Example of a Direct Dispute Request (Format)

I am disputing the accuracy of the information you are reporting regarding the account listed below.

- Creditor Name:
- Account Number:

The following information is inaccurate: [brief factual description].

Please conduct a reasonable investigation as required under the Fair Credit Reporting Act and provide documentation verifying the accuracy of this account. If the information cannot be verified, I request that it be corrected or removed from all credit bureaus to which you report.

Short. Professional. Effective.

Where to Send Direct Disputes

Send disputes to:

- The creditor's dispute address (often on statements or website)
- Not the payment address
- Not customer service

Many large creditors have dedicated compliance or dispute departments. Sending it to the wrong place slows everything down.

Certified Mail Is Your Friend

For direct disputes, certified mail is strongly recommended.

Why:

- Proof of receipt
- Legal paper trail
- Clear timeline

This isn't about intimidation. It's about documentation.

How Long Furnishers Have to Respond

Furnishers generally have:

About 30 days to investigate and respond

They must:

- Correct inaccurate data
- Stop reporting unverifiable data

- Notify bureaus of changes

Silence is not compliance.

Common Mistakes to Avoid

Please don't:

- Admit the debt while disputing accuracy
- Combine multiple accounts in one letter
- Argue fairness instead of facts
- Send incomplete documentation
- Dispute everything at once

Precision wins.

What Happens After a Successful Direct Dispute

If the furnisher agrees:

- They correct their records
- They notify all bureaus
- The change flows across reports

This is often faster than bureau-only disputes.

The Takeaway

Disputing directly with creditors and data furnishers cuts out the middleman and forces accountability. When used at the right time and with the right documentation, it's one of the most powerful tools in credit repair.

Next, we'll dive into the Section 623 method—how to demand proof that a creditor has the legal right and documentation to report a debt in the first place.

5.2 The 623 Method for Verification of Debt

This is where credit repair starts feeling less like paperwork and more like leverage.

If you've ever disputed an account, got the dreaded "verified as accurate" response, and thought, "Verified by who, exactly?"—you're already thinking in the right direction. The 623 Method exists for one simple reason: it forces creditors and collection agencies to prove they actually have the right to report what they're reporting.

After 20 years in this field, I can tell you this method doesn't work because it's aggressive. It works because it's precise and rooted in the law.

What the 623 Method Actually Is

The 623 Method is named after Section 623 of the Fair Credit Reporting Act, which governs the responsibilities of data furnishers—the companies reporting information to the credit bureaus.

In plain English, this section says:

- Furnishers must report accurate information
- Furnishers must investigate disputes
- Furnishers must correct or delete information that cannot be verified
- The 623 Method is not about saying "this isn't mine."
- It's about saying: "Prove you have the documentation and legal authority to report this."

Big difference.

Why This Method Is So Effective

Here's something most people don't realize:

many creditors and collection agencies do not have full documentation, especially on older accounts.

Debts get:

- Sold
- Transferred
- Assigned
- Bundled
- Resold

By the time a collection shows up on your report, the paper trail is often thin. The 623 Method exposes that weakness.

If they can't verify the debt properly, they cannot legally keep reporting it.

When the 623 Method Works Best

This method is most effective when:

- A dispute with the bureau has already failed
- The account is a collection or charge-off
- The debt is several years old
- Ownership of the debt is unclear
- Dates or balances seem questionable

It's less effective for:

- Brand-new accounts

- Active accounts in good standing
- Debts with complete, well-documented histories

This is a scalpel, not a hammer.

What You Are Asking for Under Section 623

You are not asking for favors. You are requesting verification.

Specifically, you're asking the furnisher to confirm:

- They have the authority to report the account
- The account belongs to you
- The balance is accurate
- The dates being reported are correct

The information was verified during a reasonable investigation

If they can't confirm those things, the law requires correction or removal.

How This Differs from Debt Validation

People confuse the 623 Method with debt validation under the Fair Debt Collection Practices Act. They are not the same.

Debt validation:

- Applies mainly to collection agencies
- Focuses on the right to collect

The 623 Method:

- Applies to all furnishers
- Focuses on the right to report

You can owe a debt and still have it removed if it's being reported incorrectly or without proper verification.

That sentence alone is worth rereading.

How to Write a 623 Verification Request

This letter should be:

- Direct
- Professional
- Calm
- Very specific

You are requesting proof, not arguing your case.

Sample 623 Method Letter (Format)

I am writing to request verification of the information you are reporting to the credit bureaus regarding the account listed below.

- Creditor/Collection Agency Name:
- Account Number:

Under Section 623 of the Fair Credit Reporting Act, you are required to report accurate and verifiable information. Please provide documentation verifying that this account is accurate, that you have the legal authority to report it, and that a reasonable investigation was conducted.

If you are unable to verify this information, please correct or remove the account from all credit bureaus to which you report.

Please respond in writing with the results of your investigation.

Notice what's missing:

- No admissions
- No emotional language
- No threats

Just obligations.

Where to Send a 623 Request

Send it directly to:

- The creditor or collection agency
- Their dispute or compliance address
- Not customer service
- Not the payment address

Always send this by certified mail. Always.

This letter is useless without a paper trail.

What a Valid Response Looks Like

A real response should include:

- Documentation
- Account records
- Proof of ownership
- Clear verification

What you'll often get instead:

- Generic statements
- Computer-generated summaries

- No actual proof

Generic responses are not verification.

What to Do If They Don't Respond (Or Respond Poorly)

If the furnisher:

- Doesn't respond
- Responds without documentation
- Ignores the request

You now have leverage.

At that point, you can:

- Dispute again with the bureaus citing lack of verification
- Escalate with certified follow-ups
- File complaints with regulators
- Document compliance failures

Silence or vague responses strengthen your position.

A Common Mistake to Avoid

Do not use the 623 Method as your first move. It works best after:

- Initial bureau disputes
- Documentation review
- Error identification

Used too early, it's easy to dismiss. Used strategically, it's powerful.

The Takeaway

The 623 Method shifts the burden where it belongs—onto the company reporting the debt. When they can't prove accuracy, the law is on your side.

In the next section, we'll talk about escalation strategies—what to do when companies refuse to cooperate and how to apply pressure without crossing legal or ethical lines.

5.3 Escalating Disputes When Initial Attempts Fail

This is the stage where credit repair stops being polite and starts being effective.

If you've disputed through the credit bureaus, disputed directly with the furnisher, used the 623 Method, and still keep getting brushed off, you're not doing anything wrong. You've just reached the point where escalation becomes necessary.

After 20 years in this field, I can tell you this: companies don't ignore disputes because they're confident. They ignore them because most people quit. Escalation works because it signals that you're not most people.

Let's talk about how to apply pressure the right way.

First: What Escalation Is (and Isn't)

Escalation is not:

- Threatening lawsuits
- Yelling at customer service
- Spamming disputes
- Becoming emotional

Escalation is:

- Increasing accountability
- Expanding the audience
- Creating compliance risk

- Building a documented paper trail

The goal is to make ignoring you more inconvenient than fixing the problem.

Step One: Confirm You've Earned the Right to Escalate

Before escalating, make sure:

- You disputed accurately
- You documented errors properly
- You gave them time to respond
- You kept records

Escalation without groundwork looks reckless. Escalation with documentation looks serious.

Step Two: Use Certified Mail Strategically

If you haven't already, this is where certified mail becomes non-negotiable.

Send follow-up disputes:

- Referencing previous dispute dates
- Citing lack of proper verification
- Requesting compliance with the FCRA

Certified mail:

- Proves receipt
- Establishes timelines
- Signals legal awareness

You're not threatening action—you're documenting it.

Step Three: Expand the Dispute Audience

When one channel fails, add another.

This can include:

- Credit bureaus (again, with new context)
- Data furnishers
- Original creditors
- Compliance departments

Multiple documented touchpoints increase scrutiny.

Step Four: File a Complaint With the CFPB

This is where things often change.

A Consumer Financial Protection Bureau complaint:

- Forces a written response
- Requires explanation
- Gets reviewed by compliance teams, not customer service

These complaints don't disappear into a void. Companies track them. Regulators watch them.

Use this when:

- Errors persist
- Verification is weak or nonexistent
- Companies ignore your rights

Be factual. Attach documentation. Keep it professional.

Step Five: Contact State Regulators if Necessary

In stubborn cases, additional pressure can come from:

- State attorneys general
- State consumer protection offices

This is not about revenge—it's about oversight.

Most companies would rather correct an account than answer multiple regulatory inquiries.

Step Six: Leverage Non-Compliance

If a furnisher:

- Fails to respond
- Responds without verification
- Continues reporting unverifiable data

That's not just annoying—it can be a violation.

At this stage:

- Document everything
- Reference compliance failures in follow-ups
- Increase pressure methodically

Consistency matters more than aggression.

Step Seven: Know When Legal Consultation Makes Sense

You don't need a lawyer for most credit repair, but sometimes it's appropriate.

Consider consultation when:

- Clear FCRA violations exist
- Errors persist after escalation
- Financial harm is documented

Many consumer rights attorneys offer free consultations. Knowledge is leverage.

The Biggest Escalation Mistake

People escalate emotionally instead of strategically.

Anger gets ignored. Documentation gets attention.

What Escalation Usually Achieves

In my experience, escalation often results in:

- Faster responses
- Deeper investigations
- Corrections that didn't happen before
- Removal of weakly documented accounts

Not always—but often enough to be worth it.

The Takeaway

Escalation isn't about being difficult. It's about being persistent, informed, and impossible to dismiss. When initial attempts fail, escalation is how you keep the process moving forward.

In the next section, we'll talk about using certified mail to build legally meaningful paper trails that protect you and strengthen every dispute you send.

5.4 Using Certified Mail for Paper Trail Documentation

If credit repair had a power move, this would be it.

Certified mail is not flashy. It doesn't guarantee results. It won't magically fix your credit overnight. But after 20 years in this field, I can tell you with absolute certainty: nothing changes the tone of a dispute faster than certified mail.

Why? Because it turns "I sent something" into "I can prove you received this on this date." And in the credit world, dates and proof matter more than opinions.

What Certified Mail Actually Does

Certified mail:

- Confirms delivery
- Provides a receipt
- Creates a legal record
- Establishes timelines

It doesn't threaten anyone. It simply removes plausible deniability.

Once something is sent certified, companies know you're documenting compliance—not asking for help.

When Certified Mail Is Worth Using

You do not need to use certified mail for every dispute. Use it strategically.

Best times to use certified mail:

- Direct disputes with creditors or collection agencies
- Section 623 verification requests
- Follow-ups after a dispute denial
- Escalation attempts
- Situations involving identity theft or fraud
- Any time deadlines matter

Online disputes are convenient. Certified mail is powerful.

What to Send by Certified Mail

Certified mail is best reserved for:

- Formal dispute letters
- Verification requests
- Escalation notices
- Documentation-heavy disputes

Do not use it for:

- Casual questions
- Payment correspondence
- General complaints

If it wouldn't matter in court, it doesn't need to be certified.

How to Send Certified Mail the Right Way

Here's the professional process:

- Print your letter

- Attach supporting documents (copies only)
- Make a complete copy of everything for yourself
- Send via certified mail with return receipt
- Track delivery
- File the receipt with your records

Yes, it costs a few dollars. It's worth it.

Why Return Receipts Matter

The return receipt shows:

- Who signed for the mail
- When it was delivered

That signature matters more than you think. It ties your dispute to a specific date and department.

If deadlines are missed after that, it's no longer ambiguous.

How Certified Mail Strengthens Deadlines

Under the Fair Credit Reporting Act, timelines matter.

Certified mail:

- Establishes when the clock starts
- Prevents "we never received it" excuses
- Supports escalation if deadlines are ignored

Without proof of receipt, deadlines become negotiable. With proof, they don't.

Common Certified Mail Mistakes to Avoid

I've seen people waste good disputes with these errors:

- Sending originals instead of copies
- Forgetting to keep copies
- Sending to the wrong address
- Mailing to customer service instead of compliance
- Using certified mail without proper documentation

Certified mail amplifies good preparation. It doesn't fix bad preparation.

Where to Find the Right Address

Always send certified disputes to:

- The creditor's dispute or compliance address
- Not the payment address
- Not the call center address

If you're unsure, check:

- Recent statements
- Company websites
- Credit report dispute address listings

Wrong address = delayed response.

What Happens After You Send Certified Mail

Typically:

- Response times improve
- Tone becomes more formal

- Compliance departments get involved
- Issues are taken more seriously

Not always—but often enough to make a difference.

Why Certified Mail Is a Psychological Shift

This isn't about intimidation. It's about clarity.

Certified mail signals:

- You know your rights
- You're keeping records
- You're prepared to escalate if needed

That alone changes how your dispute is handled.

The Takeaway

Certified mail doesn't guarantee success, but it guarantees accountability. In credit repair, accountability is everything. When you need proof, timelines, and leverage, certified mail is your best ally.

In the next section, we'll talk about when it makes sense to consider legal action or file formal complaints—and how to do so without overreacting or burning bridges.

5.5 When to Consider Legal Action or CFPB Complaints

This is the part of credit repair where people either freeze up or go nuclear too fast. Both are mistakes.

Legal action and CFPB complaints are not threats, punishments, or emotional responses. They are tools. Powerful ones. And like any good tool, they work best when used at the right time for the right reason.

After 20 years in this field, I can tell you this clearly: most credit issues never need legal action, but the ones that do tend to resolve quickly once real oversight is involved.

Let's talk about how to recognize that moment.

First: What This Step Is Really About

- You are not suing because you're angry.
- You are not filing complaints to "get revenge."

You are escalating because:

- Errors persist despite proper disputes
- Legal obligations are being ignored
- Financial harm is continuing
- Documentation is on your side

This is about accountability, not aggression.

When a CFPB Complaint Makes Sense

The Consumer Financial Protection Bureau exists for exactly this situation.

A CFPB complaint is appropriate when:

- A bureau or furnisher ignores disputes
- Responses are vague or non-responsive
- Information is "verified" without proof
- Reporting continues despite clear errors
- Deadlines are missed

These complaints:

- Require written responses
- Are reviewed by compliance teams
- Create regulatory records

This is not customer service. This is oversight.

What a Strong CFPB Complaint Includes

Keep it factual and concise.

Include:

- Timeline of disputes
- Copies of correspondence
- Proof of delivery
- Clear description of the error
- Specific compliance failure

Do not rant. Do not speculate. Do not threaten.

Professional complaints get professional responses.

What CFPB Complaints Often Achieve

In real-world practice, CFPB complaints often result in:

- Faster investigations
- Corrections that previously stalled
- Deletions of weakly documented accounts
- Clear explanations (finally)

Not always—but often enough to matter.

When to Consider Legal Consultation

Legal action should be considered when:

- Clear FCRA violations exist
- Errors remain after escalation
- Financial damage is documented
- Identity theft was mishandled
- Accounts were re-reported improperly

This doesn't mean filing a lawsuit immediately. It means talking to someone who knows the law.

Many consumer rights attorneys offer free consultations. Use them.

Signs You Might Have a Strong Case

Red flags include:

- Continued reporting after failed verification
- Ignoring certified mail

- Re-aging accounts illegally
- Re-reporting removed items without notice
- Refusing to correct obvious errors

If the law is being ignored, leverage shifts.

What Legal Action Is Not

Legal action is not:

- A quick credit fix
- A guarantee of deletion
- Something you do without preparation

It's a last-mile option, not a starting point.

Why Most People Never Need to Go This Far

Most credit issues resolve earlier because:

- Companies don't want regulatory attention
- Compliance departments intervene
- Documentation exposes weak reporting

Escalation works precisely because it's uncommon.

The Biggest Mistake at This Stage

Threatening legal action without follow-through.

Empty threats reduce credibility. Quiet preparation increases it.

The Takeaway

Legal action and CFPB complaints are not about being dramatic—they're about enforcing rights when other methods fail. When used thoughtfully and with proper documentation, they can break through stubborn resistance and bring long-running issues to an end.

In the next chapter, we'll shift focus to collections and charge-offs and show you how to deal with them strategically instead of emotionally.

Chapter 6: Dealing with Collections and Charge-Offs

Few things in life are as annoying as collection agencies. They call at dinner time. They send threatening letters. They act like you personally insulted their ancestors by missing a payment on a medical bill from 2019. I once had a collector tell me my debt had "grown" due to interest and fees - like it was some kind of financial Chia Pet. Here's what they don't tell you: collection agencies buy old debts for pennies on the dollar, which means they have way less power than they pretend to have. Most of them can't even prove they own the debt they're collecting. And that charge-off on your report? It's negotiable. Everything is negotiable. These accounts feel permanent and terrifying, but they're actually some of the easiest negative items to handle once you know the rules they're legally required to follow.

This chapter addresses the specific challenges posed by collection accounts and charge-offs on your credit report. You will learn how these negative items impact your credit score and for how long they legally remain on your report. We will cover debt validation procedures that require collection agencies to prove their legal right to collect and the accuracy of the amount claimed. This chapter provides negotiation strategies for pay-for-delete agreements, where collectors remove the negative item in exchange for payment. You will understand settlement tactics for paying less than the full amount owed and learn about statute of limitations laws that protect you from legal action on time-barred debts, sometimes called zombie debts.

6.1 Understanding How Collections Damage Your Credit

Few things feel as discouraging as seeing a collection account on your credit report. It doesn't matter if it's $87 or $8,700—it hits your stomach the same way. After 20 years in this field, I've watched people panic, pay the first collector who calls, and accidentally make their situation worse. So before we talk about fixing collections, you need to understand how they actually damage your credit and why they're such a big deal.

Once you understand the mechanics, collections become a lot less scary—and a lot more manageable.

What a Collection Really Is

A collection account appears when an original creditor gives up on collecting a debt and hands it off to a collection agency or sells it outright.

That debt could be:

- Medical bills
- Credit cards
- Utilities
- Personal loans
- Old phone or internet accounts

Once an account goes to collections, it becomes a major derogatory item on your credit report.

Why Collections Hit So Hard

Collections hurt your credit in three main ways:

They signal serious default

- A collection tells lenders you didn't just miss a payment—you stopped paying altogether.

They override positive history

- You can have years of on-time payments, and one collection can still drag your score down significantly.

They affect multiple scoring factors

Collections damage:

- Payment history
- Overall risk profile
- Lender confidence

That's why the score drop from a collection can be dramatic.

How Much Does a Collection Lower Your Score?

There's no fixed number, but here's what I've seen repeatedly:

- First collection: often a 50–100 point drop
- Multiple collections: compounded damage
- Recent collections: worse than older ones

If you already have negative items, a collection still hurts—but less than if your report was otherwise clean.

New vs Old Collections (This Matters)

Collections lose power over time.

- Recent collections hurt the most

- Older collections matter less, especially after a few years

Lenders care more about what you did last year than what you did five years ago. Time is not forgiveness, but it is relief.

Paid Collections vs Unpaid Collections

This is where confusion runs wild.

Here's the truth:

- Paying a collection does not automatically remove it
- A paid collection can still hurt your score
- Some scoring models ignore paid collections, others don't

That's why strategy matters. Blindly paying collections is often a mistake.

- The goal isn't "paid."
- The goal is removed.

Medical vs Non-Medical Collections

Medical collections are treated more leniently by newer scoring models, and they often have special rules.

Still, don't ignore them. They can:

- Affect approvals
- Trigger denials
- Appear in manual underwriting reviews

Less harmful does not mean harmless.

Why Small Collections Can Hurt More Than Big Ones

This one feels unfair, but it's true.

A $50 collection can hurt your score just as much as a $5,000 one because scoring models care more about presence than amount.

Lenders see a collection as a red flag regardless of size.

How Multiple Collections Compound Damage

Each collection adds:

- Another derogatory mark
- Another risk signal
- Another obstacle to approval

Even if balances are small, multiple collections create a pattern lenders don't like.

How Long Collections Stay on Your Credit Report

Most collections remain for about seven years from the Date of First Delinquency on the original account.

Paying them does not reset the clock. Time is tied to delinquency, not activity.

A Common Mistake That Makes Collections Worse

Paying without negotiating.

I've seen people pay collections in full, feel relieved, and then realize:

- The account still reports
- The score barely moved
- The damage remains

Money gone. Problem still there.

The Takeaway

Collections damage your credit because they represent breakdowns in repayment, not because of how much you owe. Understanding how they work puts you back in control.

In the next section, we'll talk about negotiating pay-for-delete agreements—one of the most effective ways to deal with collections the right way instead of the expensive way.

6.2 Negotiating Pay-for-Delete Agreements

If there's one phrase that can instantly change how you deal with collections, it's pay for delete. Not "pay and hope." Not "pay because they're yelling." Pay for delete—meaning the collection account is removed from your credit report in exchange for payment.

After 20 years in this field, I can tell you this: pay-for-delete agreements are real, they work, and they're one of the smartest tools you have—when used correctly. They're also one of the easiest ways to waste money if you do them wrong.

Let's get this right.

What a Pay-for-Delete Agreement Is

A pay-for-delete agreement is a negotiation where:

- You agree to pay all or part of a collection
- The collection agency agrees to remove the account from your credit report

Removal means:

- Gone from all three bureaus
- Not marked "paid collection"
- Not updated as "settled"
- Actually deleted

If it's not deleted, it's not pay-for-delete.

Why Collectors Are Willing to Do This

Here's what most people don't realize: collection agencies buy debts for pennies on the dollar. That $1,000 debt might have cost them $50 to $100.

They make money if you pay anything above what they paid.

They also know:

- Old debts are harder to collect
- Reporting pressure is their main leverage
- Many consumers won't negotiate

That gives you room.

When Pay-for-Delete Works Best

Pay-for-delete is most effective when:

- The debt is several months or years old
- The collection agency owns the debt
- The balance is relatively small
- The account is hurting approvals

It's less effective with:

- Very recent collections
- Original creditors (some refuse outright)
- Certain large medical providers

Timing matters.

How Much Should You Offer?

Never start with the full amount.

Typical starting offers:

- 25%–40% of the balance for older debts
- 40%–60% for newer debts

The older the debt, the more flexible they usually are.

And yes, it's normal for them to say no at first.

How to Start the Conversation

You can negotiate by:

- Mail
- Phone
- Email

Mail creates the best paper trail. Phone is faster but riskier.

Keep it simple:

- You're willing to resolve the account
- Only in exchange for deletion
- In writing

No explanations. No apologies.

What to Say (and Not Say)

Say:

"I'm willing to settle this account in exchange for removal from my credit reports."

Do not say:

- "I know I owe this"
- "I just want this gone"
- "I'll pay if you mark it paid"

Words matter.

Always Get the Agreement in Writing

This is non-negotiable.

Before you pay:

- Get written confirmation
- Make sure it states deletion
- Keep a copy forever

If it's not in writing, it doesn't exist.

How to Pay Safely

When it's time to pay:

- Use a method you can document
- Avoid giving direct bank access
- Keep receipts and confirmations

Never assume deletion happens automatically.

What If They Refuse Pay-for-Delete?

Some collectors say no. That's reality.

If they refuse:

- Wait and try again later

- Offer less, not more
- Explore dispute or validation strategies
- Consider whether paying without deletion makes sense

Patience often works better than pressure.

A Huge Mistake to Avoid

Never pay a collection:

- Without a written agreement
- Hoping they'll "do the right thing"
- Because they threatened you

Once you pay without terms, your leverage is gone.

The Takeaway

Pay-for-delete agreements turn collections from permanent damage into negotiable problems. When done correctly, they can clean your report faster than almost anything else.

In the next section, we'll cover validating debt with collection agencies—another critical tool that often determines whether you should negotiate at all.

6.3 Validating Debt with Collection Agencies

Before you pay a collection. Before you negotiate. Before you lose sleep over a scary letter with lots of bold text and fake urgency—validate the debt.

This is one of the most misunderstood and underused tools consumers have, and after 20 years in this field, I can tell you it stops bad collections cold more often than people realize. Not because collectors are evil masterminds, but because many of them simply can't prove what they're claiming.

Let's talk about how debt validation actually works and how to use it correctly.

What Debt Validation Really Means

Debt validation is your legal right to ask a collection agency to prove:

- You owe the debt
- The amount is accurate
- They have the legal right to collect it

This right comes from the Fair Debt Collection Practices Act. It's not optional. If they want to collect, they must be able to validate.

And no, a scary letter with a balance printed on it does not count as proof.

When You Should Validate a Debt

Debt validation is most effective when:

- You don't recognize the debt
- The amount seems wrong

- The debt is old
- Ownership is unclear
- You were contacted recently
- The collection just appeared on your credit report

If you've never validated a debt before, assume nothing and validate first.

The Critical Timing Rule Most People Miss

When a collector first contacts you, you typically have 30 days to request validation.

If you request within that window:

- Collection activity must pause
- They must respond before continuing

If you request after 30 days:

- They can continue collecting
- But they still must provide validation if they want to enforce the debt

Earlier is better, but later is not useless.

What a Proper Validation Request Looks Like

Your request should be:

- Written
- Simple
- Non-admitting

You are not arguing. You are asking for proof.

Sample Debt Validation Request (Format)

I am requesting validation of the alleged debt referenced above.

Please provide documentation showing that I am legally obligated to pay this debt, including the name of the original creditor, the amount owed, and proof of your authority to collect.

Until this information is provided, I request that collection activity cease.

That's it. Short and effective.

What Counts as Proper Validation

Valid validation includes:

- Original creditor name
- Account history
- Proof of ownership or assignment
- Accurate balance breakdown

What does not count:

- A printout with your name and balance
- A screenshot of their system
- A generic letter restating the debt

If they can't produce real documentation, they're stuck.

What Happens If They Can't Validate

If a collector can't validate:

- They should stop collecting
- They should not report or continue reporting

- They often quietly disappear

This is one of the cleanest outcomes in credit repair.

How Validation Affects Your Credit Report

Debt validation focuses on collection activity, not reporting accuracy. That said:

- Unvalidated debts should not be reported
- Continued reporting without validation creates leverage
- Validation failures strengthen disputes and complaints

Validation and credit reporting strategies work best together.

A Huge Mistake to Avoid

Do not:

- Admit the debt while requesting validation
- Make payments before validation
- Provide unnecessary personal information
- Argue about fairness or hardship

Proof first. Everything else later.

Certified Mail Matters Here

Always send validation requests by certified mail.

Why:

- Proof of request
- Proof of receipt

- Proof of timeline

If things escalate, this paper trail matters.

The Takeaway

Debt validation flips the power dynamic. Instead of you proving you don't owe something, the collector has to prove you do. Many can't—and that's not your problem.

In the next section, we'll talk about settling debts for less than you owe and how to do it without resetting clocks, losing leverage, or hurting your credit more than necessary.

6.4 Settling Debts for Less Than You Owe

Let's say the debt is real. It's yours. It's valid. And no amount of disputing, validating, or negotiating for deletion is going to make it disappear. That doesn't mean you're stuck paying the full amount.

After 20 years in this field, I can tell you something most people don't realize until it's too late: almost everything in collections is negotiable. The trick is knowing when to settle, how much to offer, and how to do it without accidentally causing more damage than you're fixing.

This is how you settle debts the smart way.

What "Settling" Actually Means

Settling a debt means:

- You pay less than the full balance
- The creditor or collector agrees to accept it
- The remaining balance is forgiven

On your credit report, this usually shows as:

- "Settled"
- "Paid for less than full balance"

This is not ideal—but it's often better than leaving a debt unpaid forever.

When Settling Makes Sense

Settlement is a good option when:

- The debt is accurate

- Deletion is not possible
- Legal action is a concern
- You want closure
- You have limited funds

If the debt is old, disputed, or unverifiable, settlement may not be the best first move.

How Much Can You Settle For?

This depends on:

- Age of the debt
- Whether the collector owns it
- Balance amount
- Your negotiation patience

Typical settlement ranges I see:

- 20%–40% for very old debts
- 40%–60% for moderately aged debts
- 60%–80% for newer debts

Start low. You can always go up.

Lump Sum vs Payment Plan

Collectors prefer lump sums. You get better deals that way.

Lump sum advantages:

- Lower total amount

- Faster resolution
- Less risk of mistakes

Payment plans:

- Cost more
- Drag things out
- Increase chances of errors

If you can scrape together a lump sum, it's usually worth it.

Always Negotiate Before Paying

Never say:

- "How much do I owe?"
- "I just want to pay this off."

Instead:

- Ask what they'll accept to resolve the account
- Make offers conditional
- Stay calm and boring

Negotiation is business, not confession.

Get Everything in Writing

Before paying:

- Get written settlement terms
- Confirm the amount
- Confirm how it will be reported

- Keep the agreement

Verbal promises disappear. Paper doesn't.

How Settlement Affects Your Credit

Let's be honest.

Settlement:

- Does not erase past damage
- Looks better than unpaid collections
- Helps manual underwriting
- Helps future lenders see resolution

It's a step forward, not a reset.

A Common (and Costly) Mistake

Making a small "good faith" payment.

This can:

- Reset statute of limitations in some states
- Restart collection activity
- Kill negotiation leverage

Never send money without terms.

Tax Implications (Quick Reality Check)

Forgiven debt over certain amounts may be reported as income. This isn't always the case, but it's something to be aware of.

Don't let fear stop you—just be informed.

The Takeaway

Settling debts for less than you owe is not failure. It's strategy. When done correctly, it reduces financial stress, prevents legal risk, and moves you forward.

In the next section, we'll talk about zombie debts and statute of limitations—how old debts come back to life and how to protect yourself from paying money you no longer legally owe.

6.5 Handling Zombie Debts and Statute of Limitations

Zombie debts are called that for a reason. They're supposed to be dead, buried, and forgotten—yet somehow they keep crawling back into your life years later, usually with a threatening letter or a phone call that starts with, "This is an attempt to collect a debt..."

After 20 years in this field, I can tell you this is one of the most dangerous areas of credit repair—not because the debts are powerful, but because people accidentally bring them back to life.

Let's make sure that doesn't happen to you.

What a Zombie Debt Actually Is

A zombie debt is typically:

- Very old
- Long past its prime
- Often already written off
- Sometimes already paid, settled, or discharged
- Frequently sold multiple times

These debts resurface because:

- Debt buyers purchase old portfolios cheaply
- Records are incomplete or inaccurate
- Consumers don't remember details from years ago

The age of the debt is your biggest weapon here.

The Two Timelines That Matter (Don't Confuse Them)

This is where people get burned, so pay attention.

There are two completely different clocks involved:

- Credit Reporting Time Limit
- Usually about 7 years from the Date of First Delinquency
- Determines how long the debt can appear on your credit report
- Statute of Limitations (SOL)
- Varies by state
- Determines how long a creditor can sue you

A debt can be:

Too old to sue on

- But still showing on your credit report

Or:

- Off your credit report
- But still legally collectible (in rare cases)

Different clocks. Different rules.

What the Statute of Limitations Really Means

The statute of limitations is the legal deadline for filing a lawsuit to collect a debt.

Once it expires:

- You can no longer be sued successfully

- The debt does not magically disappear
- Collectors may still attempt to collect

But here's the key: they cannot legally force you to pay through the courts.

That changes the power dynamic completely.

The Biggest Mistake People Make With Zombie Debts

This mistake deserves its own warning label:

Making a payment or admitting the debt.

In many states, doing either can:

- Restart the statute of limitations
- Revive the creditor's right to sue
- Turn a dead debt into a live legal risk

I've seen people turn a harmless old debt into a lawsuit over a $25 "good faith" payment. Don't be that person.

How Zombie Debts Usually Reappear

Common tactics include:

- Letters implying urgency
- Phone calls referencing "pending action"
- Settlement offers "for a limited time"
- Threats that sound legal but aren't

Collectors rely on fear and confusion, not facts.

How to Identify a Zombie Debt

Ask these questions:

- When was the last payment actually made?
- When did the account first go delinquent?
- Is this past the reporting period?
- Is it past the statute of limitations in my state?

If you don't know the answers, do nothing until you find out.

Silence is safer than guessing.

What You Should Do If Contacted About a Zombie Debt

Here's the safe approach:

- Do not admit the debt
- Do not make a payment
- Do not agree to anything verbally
- Request written communication
- Validate the debt
- Check the statute of limitations

You are allowed to ask questions. You are not required to help them.

How Zombie Debts Affect Your Credit

If a zombie debt:

- Is past reporting limits, it should not be on your report
- Reappears with a new date, that's illegal re-aging
- Is reported inaccurately, it's disputable

Old debt does not get a second life on your credit report just because it was sold again.

When to Dispute vs When to Ignore

Dispute when:

- It's reporting illegally
- Dates are wrong
- It shouldn't be on your report

Ignore (strategically) when:

- It's off your report
- It's past the statute of limitations
- Contact is minimal and manageable

Not every old debt needs engagement.

Why Patience Wins With Zombie Debts

Zombie debt collectors thrive on reaction. The less you give them—emotionally, verbally, financially—the less leverage they have.

Knowledge, not money, is your strongest defense here.

The Takeaway

Zombie debts are only dangerous if you revive them. Once you understand reporting timelines and statute of limitations rules, fear disappears and control returns. Old debts don't get to haunt you forever—unless you invite them back.

That wraps up collections. In the next chapter, we'll move into strategic debt paydown methods—how to deal with the debts you actually owe in a way that helps your credit instead of quietly sabotaging it.

Chapter 7: Strategic Debt Paydown Methods

Let's talk about the elephant in the room: you probably have actual debt that you actually owe, and no amount of disputing or negotiating will make it disappear. I know, disappointing. When I was staring at twelve thousand dollars in credit card debt, I felt like I'd be making minimum payments until my grandkids graduated college. Every financial guru had different advice - pay the highest interest first, pay the smallest balance first, consolidate everything, don't consolidate anything. It was exhausting. But here's what I learned after trying basically everything: the best debt paydown method is the one you'll actually stick with. Some of these strategies save you more money in interest. Others give you psychological wins that keep you motivated. The trick is matching the right method to your personality and situation, then actually executing the plan instead of just thinking about it while eating stress nachos at midnight.

This chapter presents evidence-based debt reduction strategies designed for various financial situations and psychological profiles. You will learn the debt avalanche method, which minimizes total interest paid by targeting high-interest debts first, and the debt snowball method, which builds momentum through quick wins by eliminating smallest balances first. We will develop realistic debt repayment budgets that account for actual living expenses without requiring unsustainable sacrifices. This chapter covers negotiation techniques for reducing interest rates with current creditors and analyzes when debt consolidation loans or balance transfers provide genuine benefits versus when they simply restructure problems without solving them. Implementing these strategies will accelerate your path to becoming debt-free while improving your credit profile.

7.1 The Debt Avalanche Method for Maximum Savings

If debt had a personality, high-interest debt would be the friend who borrows money and then charges you rent for thinking about it. Credit cards with 24% APR don't just sit there—they actively drain your future. That's why, from a purely mathematical standpoint, the debt avalanche method is the most efficient way to get out of debt.

After 20 years of helping people pay off everything from a couple thousand dollars to six figures, I can tell you this: the avalanche method saves the most money. Full stop. The only question is whether it fits you.

Let's break it down in real-world terms.

What the Debt Avalanche Method Is

The debt avalanche method works like this:

- List all your debts
- Order them by interest rate, highest to lowest
- Pay the minimum on every debt
- Throw every extra dollar at the highest-interest debt
- Once it's paid off, move to the next highest rate

You're "avalanche-ing" the most expensive debt first, letting gravity (math) do the rest.

Why the Avalanche Method Saves the Most Money

Interest is the enemy. The higher the rate, the more you pay for the privilege of owing money.

By attacking the highest-interest debt first:

- You reduce total interest paid
- You shorten the payoff timeline
- You stop the fastest-growing balances early

Over time, this can save thousands of dollars compared to other methods.

I've seen people shave years off their payoff plans just by switching to avalanche.

Who the Avalanche Method Works Best For

This method is ideal if:

- You're motivated by logic and numbers
- You can stay focused without quick wins
- You're carrying high-interest credit cards
- You want maximum efficiency

If you like spreadsheets, calculators, and seeing interest drop fast, this method will make you happy.

Where People Struggle With Avalanche

Here's the downside, and it's real.

The avalanche method can feel slow at first because:

- The highest-interest debt isn't always the smallest
- Progress may not be immediately visible
- You might be working on one balance for months

Mathematically satisfying doesn't always mean emotionally satisfying.

A Simple Example (Realistic Numbers)

Let's say you have:

- **Card A:** $2,000 at 26%
- **Card B:** $5,000 at 18%
- **Card C:** $1,000 at 12%

Avalanche order:

- Card A (26%)
- Card B (18%)
- Card C (12%)

Even though Card C is the smallest, you ignore it for now because it's not costing you as much.

Cold? Yes. Effective? Also yes.

How to Find Extra Money for Avalanche Payments

People ask this all the time: "Where does the extra money come from?"

Common sources:

- Temporary expense cuts
- Tax refunds
- Bonuses
- Side income
- Redirected minimum payments from paid-off debts

You don't need perfection. You need consistency.

A Credit Score Bonus You Might Not Expect

Here's something people don't talk about enough: avalanche often improves credit scores faster than you'd expect.

Why?

- High-interest cards are often maxed out
- Paying them down reduces utilization quickly
- Utilization changes can boost scores within a month

This is one of the few cases where doing the "smart" thing financially also helps your credit.

When Avalanche Might Not Be the Best Choice

Avalanche may not be ideal if:

- You're easily discouraged
- You need quick wins to stay motivated
- Your highest-interest debt is massive and slow to move

Debt payoff is a behavior problem as much as a math problem.

How to Stick With the Avalanche Method

If you choose avalanche:

- Track progress visually
- Celebrate interest savings, not just balances
- Avoid opening new debt
- Recalculate periodically

Momentum builds quietly at first, then suddenly.

The Takeaway

The debt avalanche method is the fastest, cheapest way to get out of debt—on paper. If you can stay focused through slower early wins, it will save you real money and improve your credit at the same time.

In the next section, we'll look at the debt snowball method—why it works for so many people even though it's not mathematically optimal, and how to decide which approach fits your personality better.

7.2 The Debt Snowball Method for Quick Wins

If the debt avalanche method is powered by math, the debt snowball method is powered by psychology. And before the spreadsheet crowd gets upset, let me say this clearly after 20 years of doing this: the best debt payoff method is the one you actually stick with.

I've watched people with perfect avalanche plans quit halfway through because they felt like nothing was happening. I've also watched people knock out debt after debt using the snowball method because momentum kept them going. Results beat theory every time.

Let's talk about why this method works so well for real humans.

What the Debt Snowball Method Is

The debt snowball method works like this:

- List all your debts
- Order them by balance, smallest to largest
- Pay the minimum on every debt
- Throw every extra dollar at the smallest balance
- Once it's paid off, roll that payment into the next smallest debt

Each paid-off debt adds energy to the next one—hence the "snowball."

Why the Snowball Method Works (Even When Math Says It Shouldn't)

The snowball method works because:

- Small wins feel motivating

- Progress is visible quickly
- Confidence builds with each payoff
- Fewer bills mean less stress

Debt is emotional. Motivation matters.

I've seen people wipe out five small debts in six months and suddenly believe, for the first time, that being debt-free is possible.

That belief changes behavior.

Who the Snowball Method Is Best For

This method shines if:

- You feel overwhelmed by debt
- You need early wins to stay motivated
- You've struggled to stick with plans before
- Your debts vary widely in size

If momentum fuels you, snowball is your method.

A Realistic Example

Let's say you have:

- **Card A:** $400 at 18%
- **Card B:** $1,200 at 24%
- **Card C:** $6,000 at 15%

Snowball order:

- Card A ($400)

- Card B ($1,200)
- Card C ($6,000)

Even though Card B has a higher interest rate, you ignore that at first to get a fast win.

- Is it optimal on paper? No.
- Is it effective in real life? Very often, yes.

The Psychological Boost No One Talks About

Every time you eliminate a debt:

- Your minimum payments drop
- Your stress decreases
- Your confidence increases

This creates a feedback loop. You stop feeling like debt owns you and start acting like you're in control.

That shift is powerful.

How Snowball Helps Credit Scores

Snowball can help credit in a few indirect ways:

- Reducing total balances lowers utilization
- Fewer open balances simplify management
- Less stress means fewer missed payments

It's not as targeted as avalanche, but progress is progress.

Where Snowball Falls Short

Let's be honest.

Snowball:

- Costs more in interest overall
- Can be inefficient for high-rate debt
- Takes discipline not to ignore big problems forever

That's why snowball works best when combined with awareness.

A Hybrid Approach (My Professional Favorite)

Many people do best with a hybrid strategy:

- Snowball the smallest 1–2 debts for momentum
- Switch to avalanche for the big, high-interest balances

You get quick wins and long-term savings.

This isn't cheating. It's smart.

Common Mistakes With Snowball

Avoid these:

- Adding new debt while snowballing
- Ignoring minimums on other accounts
- Using paid-off cards irresponsibly
- Quitting after the first win

Momentum only works if you protect it.

The Takeaway

The debt snowball method works because humans aren't calculators—we're emotional creatures who need visible progress to stay committed. If quick wins keep you moving, snowball can be the difference between staying stuck and getting free.

In the next section, we'll focus on creating a realistic debt repayment budget—because no method works without a plan that fits your actual life.

7.3 Creating a Realistic Debt Repayment Budget

Let's get something out of the way: if your budget only works on paper, it's not a budget—it's a fantasy novel.

After 20 years of working with real people (with real lives, real bills, and real bad months), I can tell you this with confidence: the most effective debt repayment budget is boring, flexible, and slightly forgiving. If it requires you to live like a monk, eat nothing but rice, or never have fun again, it will fail. Not because you're weak—but because you're human.

Let's build something you can actually live with.

First Rule: A Budget Is a Tool, Not a Punishment

Most people avoid budgeting because they associate it with restriction and guilt. That mindset kills progress.

A good debt repayment budget:

- Tells your money where to go
- Reduces decision fatigue
- Protects you from surprise stress
- Creates consistency, not perfection

You're not trying to "win" a month. You're trying to repeat decent behavior over many months.

Step One: Start With Reality, Not Goals

Before you plan where money should go, you need to see where it is going.

Track one full month of:

- Income (after taxes)
- Fixed expenses
- Variable expenses
- Debt minimums
- Random "where did this go?" spending

No judgment. No editing. This is reconnaissance, not confession.

Most people are shocked—not because they're irresponsible, but because small leaks add up fast.

Step Two: Separate Fixed and Flexible Expenses

Break expenses into two categories:

Fixed expenses

- Rent or mortgage
- Utilities
- Insurance
- Minimum debt payments
- Phone, internet

Transportation basics

Flexible expenses

- Groceries
- Dining out
- Entertainment
- Subscriptions

- Miscellaneous spending

You don't attack fixed expenses first. You manage flexible ones.

Step Three: Pay Yourself Breathing Room First

This is where most budgets quietly fail.

You must include:

- A small buffer
- Emergency padding
- "Life happens" money

Even $50–$100 per month set aside prevents:

- New debt
- Missed payments
- Emotional spending blowups

A budget with no margin breaks under pressure.

Step Four: Lock in Minimum Payments Automatically

Your budget must protect your credit while you repay debt.

Do this immediately:

- Set autopay for minimums on all debts
- Align due dates if possible
- Remove willpower from the equation

Minimums keep accounts current. Extra payments are where progress happens.

Step Five: Decide Your Debt Attack Number

This is the most important number in your budget.

Ask:

- How much can I consistently apply toward debt each month?

Not on a perfect month—on an average one

This number:

- Funds avalanche or snowball strategies
- Should feel slightly uncomfortable
- Should not cause burnout

Consistency beats intensity.

Step Six: Build the Budget Around Your Pay Schedule

Monthly budgets fail for people paid biweekly or weekly.

Instead:

- Budget per paycheck
- Assign jobs to money as it arrives
- Avoid spending "future" money early

This reduces overdrafts, missed payments, and stress.

Step Seven: Cut Strategically, Not Emotionally

You don't need to cut everything. You need to cut enough.

High-impact cuts often include:

- Subscriptions you forgot about

- Convenience spending
- Impulse food purchases
- Upgrading plans you don't need

Low-impact cuts:

- Essentials
- Anything that keeps you sane

If your budget makes you miserable, it will not survive.

Step Eight: Plan for Irregular Expenses

Real life includes:

- Car repairs
- Gifts
- Medical costs
- Travel
- Annual fees

Set aside small amounts monthly so these don't become debt again.

Surprises aren't surprising if you plan for them.

Step Nine: Review Monthly, Adjust Guilt-Free

Your budget should evolve.

Each month:

- Review what worked
- Identify friction points

- Adjust numbers honestly

A budget that adapts survives. One that demands perfection collapses.

Common Budgeting Mistakes to Avoid

Please don't:

- Assume next month will be cheaper
- Ignore irregular expenses
- Cut joy completely
- Use debt as a backup plan
- Quit after one bad month

Bad months happen. Quitting is optional.

The Takeaway

A realistic debt repayment budget doesn't require extreme discipline—it requires honest math, flexible thinking, and compassion for yourself. When your budget fits your life, debt payoff stops feeling like punishment and starts feeling like progress.

In the next section, we'll talk about negotiating lower interest rates with creditors—one of the fastest ways to make your budget work harder without earning another dollar.

7.4 Negotiating Lower Interest Rates with Creditors

This might be one of the most underused tools in personal finance, mostly because people assume it won't work. They picture a bank laughing, hanging up, and adding a penalty APR just for asking. That's not how it usually goes.

After 20 years in this field, I can tell you this: creditors lower interest rates all the time. Not out of kindness, but because keeping a paying customer at a lower rate is often better than losing them to default, balance transfers, or bankruptcy.

You don't need leverage, threats, or a perfect credit score. You need timing, a calm voice, and the right words.

Why Creditors Are Willing to Negotiate

Here's the logic from the creditor's side:

- You're already paying
- You haven't defaulted
- Losing you costs them money
- Charging slightly less interest still earns profit

Credit card companies especially expect these calls. They have departments for them.

You're not asking for a favor—you're asking for a retention adjustment.

When Negotiating Rates Works Best

Your odds improve if:

- You've made on-time payments consistently
- Your account is in good standing
- You've had the card for a while
- Your credit has improved since opening

Even if only one or two of these apply, it's worth trying.

What You Can Actually Ask For

You can request:

- A temporary APR reduction
- A permanent APR reduction
- Removal of a penalty APR
- Promotional rates

Start with permanent. Settle for temporary if needed.

Temporary reductions often last 6–12 months and can save hundreds in interest.

The Best Way to Make the Call

Call the number on the back of your card and ask for:

- The retention department
- Or a supervisor if needed

Be polite. Calm. Boring.

This is a business conversation, not a confrontation.

What to Say (This Matters)

Here's a script that works shockingly well:

- "I've been a customer for a while and I've been working hard to pay down my balance. The interest rate is making it difficult. I'd like to know if there's anything you can do to lower my APR."

That's it.

No threats. No ultimatums. No long stories.

What If They Say No?

No doesn't always mean no.

Try:

- Asking again politely
- Calling back another day
- Asking for a temporary reduction
- Mentioning competitive offers (without bluffing)

Different reps have different authority.

How Much Can Rates Drop?

I've seen:

- 3%–6% permanent reductions
- 0%–10% temporary reductions
- Penalty APRs removed entirely

Even a few percentage points make a real difference over time.

A Credit Score Bonus You Might Not Expect

Lower interest rates:

- Help balances fall faster
- Reduce utilization sooner
- Improve credit scores indirectly

This is one of the rare moves that helps cash flow and credit at the same time.

When Negotiation Is Less Likely to Work

It's harder if:

- You're already delinquent
- The account is brand new
- The balance is extremely high relative to limit

Even then, asking costs nothing.

Common Mistakes to Avoid

Please don't:

- Threaten bankruptcy
- Mention hardship unless asked
- Accept the first no as final
- Feel embarrassed for asking

You're not begging. You're negotiating.

How Often You Can Ask

There's no penalty for asking, but don't call weekly.

Reasonable cadence:

- Once every 6–12 months

- After major credit improvements
- After balance reductions

Persistence beats pressure.

The Takeaway

Negotiating lower interest rates is one of the easiest ways to make debt payoff faster without earning more or cutting deeper. One phone call can save months—or years—of unnecessary interest.

In the next section, we'll talk about when debt consolidation actually makes sense and when it just reshuffles the problem instead of solving it.

7.5 When Debt Consolidation Makes Sense

Debt consolidation gets marketed like a miracle cure. One payment. One interest rate. One clean slate. And sometimes—sometimes—it really does help. Other times, it's just moving the mess from one room to another and calling it "organized."

After 20 years in this field, I've seen consolidation work beautifully, and I've seen it quietly make things worse. The difference isn't the product—it's the timing, the math, and the behavior behind it.

Let's talk about when consolidation actually makes sense, and when it's a trap wearing a suit.

What Debt Consolidation Really Is

At its core, debt consolidation means:

- Taking multiple debts
- Combining them into one new loan or balance
- Ideally at a lower interest rate

That's it. No magic. No forgiveness. No disappearance of debt.

If the total amount owed doesn't go down or the interest doesn't improve, consolidation is just rearranging numbers.

The Main Types of Debt Consolidation

You'll usually see consolidation offered as:

- Personal loans
- Balance transfer credit cards

- Home equity loans or HELOCs
- Debt management plans (not the same as settlement)

Each has pros and serious cons. None are automatic wins.

When Debt Consolidation Actually Makes Sense

Consolidation can be smart if most or all of the following are true:

- Your credit score qualifies you for a lower interest rate
- You're paying high interest on multiple cards
- You're current on payments
- You have a clear payoff plan
- You will not run balances back up

That last point is the deal-breaker for most people.

If consolidation frees up cards and you immediately start using them again, you didn't solve anything—you doubled the problem.

The Math Test (Non-Negotiable)

Before consolidating, run this test:

- Is the new interest rate lower than the weighted average of your current rates?
- Is the repayment term reasonable?
- Will total interest paid be less?

If the answer to any of those is no, stop.

Lower monthly payments alone are not a win if they cost you more over time.

Balance Transfers: Powerful but Dangerous

Balance transfer cards can be great if:

- You qualify for a true 0% promo
- The transfer fee is reasonable
- You can pay it off before the promo ends

They are dangerous if:

- You treat the freed-up cards as spending money
- You miss a payment and lose the promo rate
- You underestimate how fast time passes

0% interest only works if you actually move.

Personal Loans: Structure Without Discipline

Personal loans help people who:

- Need fixed payments
- Want an end date
- Struggle with revolving credit

They hurt people who:

- Consolidate and then reuse credit cards
- Take longer terms just to lower payments
- Ignore total interest cost

Structure helps behavior—but only if behavior cooperates.

Home Equity: High Risk, High Stakes

Using home equity to consolidate consumer debt is serious.

Pros:

- Lower interest rates
- Large balances possible

Cons:

- You're turning unsecured debt into secured debt
- Your home is now on the line
- One bad year can escalate fast

I only recommend this in very specific, stable situations.

When Consolidation Does NOT Make Sense

Consolidation is usually a bad idea if:

- Your credit is already struggling
- You're behind on payments
- The interest rate isn't meaningfully lower
- You're using it to avoid budgeting
- You haven't addressed spending habits

Debt consolidation does not fix behavior. It magnifies it.

The Psychological Trap Nobody Talks About

Consolidation often creates a false sense of progress.

People think:

- "I handled it"
- "It's under control now"

- "I deserve a break"

Then balances creep back in.

If you consolidate, you must mentally treat old cards as closed—even if they're technically open.

A Smarter Alternative for Many People

For many readers, this works better:

- Pay down one or two cards aggressively
- Negotiate interest rates
- Use avalanche or snowball
- Reassess consolidation later

Consolidation is often most effective after progress has already started.

The One Question to Ask Yourself First

Before consolidating, ask this honestly:

- "If nothing else changed in my habits, would this still work?"

If the answer is no, consolidation isn't the solution yet.

The Takeaway

Debt consolidation makes sense when it lowers interest, shortens your timeline, and supports better habits—not when it just makes payments feel nicer. Used correctly, it's a tool. Used blindly, it's a delay.

That wraps up strategic debt paydown. In the next chapter, we'll shift into credit utilization management—one of the fastest ways to boost your score without paying off all your debt first.

Chapter 8: Managing Credit Utilization

Here's a fun fact that nobody told me until I was already drowning: you can have perfect payment history and still have a terrible credit score. How? Credit utilization, that sneaky little metric that accounts for thirty percent of your score. I was using ninety percent of my available credit and wondering why my score wouldn't budge despite never missing a payment. It's like being a straight-A student who fails the class because you didn't know participation counted. The worst part? I had the money to pay down the balances, I just didn't know the timing mattered. Turns out, when you pay your credit card bill makes almost as much difference as whether you pay it. Once I figured out this utilization game, my score jumped forty points in a single month. Forty points. For basically just rearranging when I paid my bills.

This chapter focuses on credit utilization ratio, the second most influential factor in credit score calculations after payment history. You will understand why maintaining utilization below thirty percent is crucial and how different utilization levels impact your score differently. We will explore strategies for reducing utilization without necessarily paying off entire balances, including optimal payment timing relative to statement closing dates and due dates. This chapter covers techniques for requesting credit limit increases that lower your utilization percentage without requiring additional payments. You will learn how utilization is calculated both per-card and across all accounts, enabling you to strategically manage balances for maximum score improvement with minimum financial resources required.

8.1 Why Credit Utilization Matters More Than You Think

Here's one of the most frustrating truths about credit: you can pay every bill on time, never miss a due date, do "everything right," and still have a mediocre credit score. I know because I lived it. Perfect payment history. Zero late payments. Still stuck. The culprit? Credit utilization.

After 20 years in this field, I can say this without hesitation: credit utilization is the most misunderstood and most powerful lever you can pull for fast score improvement. Not eventually. Fast.

Let's talk about why.

What Credit Utilization Actually Is (In Plain English)

Credit utilization is the percentage of your available revolving credit that you're using.

The formula is simple:

- Balance ÷ Credit limit = Utilization

If you have a credit card with:

- $1,000 limit
- $700 balance
- Your utilization on that card is 70%.

This applies in two ways:

- Per card utilization
- Total utilization across all cards

Both matter.

Why Utilization Carries So Much Weight

Credit utilization makes up about 30% of your credit score, second only to payment history. That's not an accident.

From a lender's perspective, utilization answers one key question:

"How close is this person to maxing out their credit?"

High utilization signals:

- Financial stress
- Higher default risk
- Dependency on credit

Even if you've never missed a payment.

Why On-Time Payments Can't Save You Here

This part hurts, but it's important.

- Paying on time tells lenders you're reliable.
- High utilization tells lenders you're stretched.

Between the two, the system is more scared of "stretched."

That's why someone with:

- One late payment five years ago
- Low balances

Can sometimes outscore someone with:

- Perfect payment history

- Maxed-out cards

It's not fair—but it is how the system works.

The Thresholds That Quietly Control Your Score

Utilization isn't graded on a smooth curve. It's broken into buckets.

While models vary, here's what generally happens:

- **Under 10%** – Excellent
- **10%–29%** – Very good
- **30%–49%** – Starting to hurt
- **50%–74%** – Significant damage
- **75%+** – Severe impact

Crossing 30% is the big one. That's where scores often stall or drop.

This is why people feel "stuck" at certain score ranges.

Why Per-Card Utilization Matters More Than You Expect

Here's a surprise for most people: you can have low total utilization and still be hurting your score.

Example:

- **Total limits:** $10,000
- **Total balance**: $2,000 (20% overall)
- Sounds good, right?

But if:

- One card is maxed at 95%

- Others are low or zero

That single card can drag your score down.

High utilization on any individual card is a red flag.

Why Utilization Is the Fastest Score Mover

Unlike late payments or collections, utilization has no memory.

That's huge.

If you lower balances before the next report:

- Your score can rebound within 30–45 days
- No waiting years
- No "credit forgiveness" required

I've seen 20-, 30-, even 40-point jumps from utilization changes alone.

Few other factors work that fast.

Why "I Pay It Off Every Month" Still Isn't Enough

This is where timing matters (we'll go deeper soon).

If you:

- Use most of your limit during the month
- Let the statement close with a high balance
- Then pay in full by the due date

Your report still shows high utilization.

The system doesn't care that you paid it later. It only sees what was reported.

That misunderstanding costs people years of slow progress.

A Common Trap: Multiple Small Balances

People often think:

- "I'll just spread balances across cards."

That can backfire if:

- Multiple cards are over 30%
- No card looks "low risk"

Fewer cards with low balances usually score better than many cards with moderate ones.

Why Utilization Feels So Unfair

Utilization punishes behavior that's technically responsible:

- Using credit as intended
- Paying on time
- Paying in full

But credit scoring isn't about responsibility. It's about risk prediction.

Once you accept that, the frustration turns into strategy.

The Takeaway

Credit utilization matters more than you think because it's immediate, powerful, and completely under your control once you understand how it works. You don't need to be debt-free to improve your score—you need to look less risky at the right moment.

In the next section, we'll break down the famous 30 percent rule, what it gets right, what it gets wrong, and how to use utilization ratios strategically instead of blindly.

8.2 The 30 Percent Rule and Optimal Utilization Ratios

If you've spent more than five minutes reading about credit online, you've heard this phrase: "Keep your utilization under 30 percent." It's everywhere. It's repeated like gospel. And while it's not wrong, it's also incomplete.

After 20 years in this field, I can tell you the 30 percent rule is more like a speed limit sign—it keeps you out of trouble, but it won't get you to the finish line. If you want strong scores, approvals, and leverage, you need to understand what optimal utilization actually looks like.

Let's clear this up.

Where the 30 Percent Rule Comes From

The 30 percent rule exists because credit scoring models start penalizing utilization noticeably once you cross that threshold.

Below 30 percent:

- You look manageable
- Risk appears contained

Above 30 percent:

- Risk models start raising eyebrows
- Scores often stall or dip

So yes, under 30 percent is better than over 30 percent—but that's just the entry level.

Why 30 Percent Is Not the Goal

Here's the part most people miss:

- Under 30 percent is "acceptable."
- Under 10 percent is "excellent."

There is a meaningful scoring difference between:

- 28 percent utilization
- 8 percent utilization

Both follow the "rule," but only one maximizes your score potential.

Utilization Is Graded in Ranges, Not Smoothly

Utilization doesn't work like a dimmer switch. It works like stairs.

While exact breakpoints vary, common tiers look like this:

- **0%** – Neutral (sometimes slightly worse than low usage)
- **1%–9%** – Optimal
- **10%–29%** – Very good
- **30%–49%** – Negative impact
- **50%–74%** – Major impact
- **75%+** – Severe damage

This is why dropping from 35% to 28% often boosts a score—but dropping from 15% to 8% can also do it.

The Per-Card Rule Most People Ignore

Total utilization gets all the attention, but per-card utilization quietly does a lot of damage.

Best practice:

- Keep each card under 30 percent
- Ideally under 10 percent on most cards
- Avoid maxing out any single card

One card at 90 percent can hurt more than three cards at 20 percent.

Why 0 Percent Utilization Isn't Perfect Either

This one surprises people.

Using no revolving credit at all can sometimes:

- Slightly suppress scores
- Make activity look dormant

Scoring models like to see responsible use—not avoidance.

That's why:

- One small balance (1%–5%)
- Paid on time

Often scores better than zero across the board.

Optimal Utilization by Credit Goal

Different goals favor different utilization targets:

- **General credit health:** under 30%
- **Score optimization:** under 10%
- **Major loan applications:** 1%–5%
- **Rebuilding credit:** as low as possible

Context matters.

Why Utilization Is Both Powerful and Fragile

Utilization is:

- Easy to improve
- Easy to mess up

A single large purchase right before a statement closes can undo months of progress.

This is why awareness matters more than obsession.

A Common Misuse of the 30 Percent Rule

People treat 30 percent like a license to spend.

- "I'm under 30%, so I'm good."
- That mindset keeps scores stuck in the "pretty good" zone instead of pushing them into "excellent."

How to Use the Rule Strategically

Use 30 percent as:

- A warning line, not a target
- A guardrail, not a goal
- A fallback, not a finish

If you want faster progress, aim lower when possible.

The Takeaway

The 30 percent rule keeps you safe, but optimal utilization gets you ahead. Once you understand that utilization is about ranges, not just limits, you can control one of the fastest-moving parts of your credit score with precision instead of guesswork.

In the next section, we'll get tactical and talk about lowering utilization without paying off all your debt—yes, that's possible, and yes, it works.

8.3 Strategies to Lower Utilization Without Paying Off Debt

This is the section where most people lean forward and say, "Wait... that's possible?"

Yes. It is. And after 20 years in this field, I can tell you that some of the fastest credit score improvements I've ever seen came from lowering utilization without eliminating debt. Not cheating. Not gaming the system. Just understanding how the system measures risk.

You don't need to be debt-free to look low-risk. You need to look low-risk at the right moment.

Let's get practical.

Strategy #1: Pay Before the Statement Closing Date (Not the Due Date)

This is the single most important tactic most people never learn.

Your credit card has:

- A statement closing date (when the balance is reported)
- A payment due date (when payment is required)

Credit bureaus see the balance on the statement date, not what you owe after you pay later.

If you:

- Pay before the statement closes
- Reduce the reported balance

Your utilization drops immediately—even if you still owe money afterward.

This one change alone can move scores in 30 days.

Strategy #2: Target One Card at a Time

You don't need to lower all balances at once.

Focus on:

- Cards over 30%
- Especially cards over 50%
- Especially especially cards near maxed out

Dropping one card from 90% to 40% can do more for your score than paying a little on five cards.

Per-card utilization matters more than people realize.

Strategy #3: Redistribute Balances (Carefully)

If you have multiple cards, you may be able to:

- Shift balances from a high-utilization card
- To a lower-utilization card

This does not reduce total debt, but it:

- Improves utilization ratios
- Reduces red flags
- Can raise scores quickly

Important caveats:

- Watch balance transfer fees
- Don't max out the receiving card

- Don't do this repeatedly

This is a tactical move, not a lifestyle.

Strategy #4: Request a Credit Limit Increase

This is one of the cleanest utilization fixes.

If your balance stays the same but your limit increases:

- Utilization drops instantly
- No payment required

Example:

- $3,000 balance on $5,000 limit = 60%
- Same balance on $8,000 limit = 37.5%

Same debt. Better score.

Best practices:

- Ask after on-time payment history
- Ask when income is stable
- Ask lenders that don't hard-pull if possible

Even a modest increase helps.

Strategy #5: Pay Down Just Enough to Cross Thresholds

You don't need to pay off cards—you need to cross utilization breakpoints.

Focus on:

- Getting below 75%
- Then below 50%

- Then below 30%
- Then below 10%

Each threshold can trigger score movement.

Paying $300 to move from 31% to 29% often helps more than paying $1,000 randomly.

Precision beats effort.

Strategy #6: Keep One Card Active, Others Minimal

This is counterintuitive but effective.

Often, the best setup is:

- One card reporting a small balance (1%–5%)
- Other cards reporting very low or zero balances

This shows:

- Active use
- Low risk
- Controlled behavior

Multiple cards with mid-range balances can look riskier than one controlled balance.

Strategy #7: Time Large Purchases Strategically

Life doesn't stop for credit scores, but timing helps.

If you must make a large purchase:

- Do it right after the statement closes
- Pay it down before the next closing date

This keeps the high balance from ever being reported.

It's not avoidance—it's awareness.

Strategy #8: Don't Close Cards to Fix Utilization

This deserves repeating.

Closing a card:

- Reduces available credit
- Raises utilization
- Often hurts scores

If a card has no annual fee and isn't a spending problem, keeping it open usually helps utilization long-term.

A Common Mistake That Cancels All This Out

People do everything right—then:

- Charge the card back up
- Forget the statement date
- Let balances creep again

Utilization management is ongoing, not one-and-done.

The Takeaway

Lowering utilization is about what your credit report sees, not what your bank account feels. By timing payments, managing limits, and targeting the right cards, you can improve your score without paying off every dollar of debt first.

In the next section, we'll talk about requesting credit limit increases strategically—how to ask, when to ask, and how to avoid hurting your score in the process.

8.4 Requesting Credit Limit Increases Strategically

If lowering utilization is the fastest way to boost your score, credit limit increases are the cleanest way to do it without spending money. Same balances. Bigger limits. Instant math win.

After 20 years in this field, I can tell you this is one of the most overlooked strategies—not because it's hard, but because people are afraid to ask. They assume it will hurt their score, trigger a denial, or somehow make things worse. Most of the time, it doesn't.

When done strategically, credit limit increases are low effort, high impact.

Why Credit Limit Increases Work So Well

Credit utilization is a ratio.

If the denominator (your credit limit) goes up and the numerator (your balance) stays the same, utilization drops.

That's it. No trick.

Example:

- $4,000 balance on a $6,000 limit = 67%
- Same balance on a $10,000 limit = 40%

Nothing changed financially. Everything changed mathematically.

When You Should Ask for a Credit Limit Increase

Timing matters.

Your odds are best when:

- You've made on-time payments for at least 6 months
- Your income is stable or higher than when you applied
- Your balance isn't maxed out
- Your credit score has improved recently

You don't need perfection. You need consistency.

When You Should Not Ask

Hold off if:

- You've missed payments recently
- You're carrying a balance close to the limit
- Your income has dropped
- You plan to apply for major credit soon

Asking at the wrong time can lead to denial or a hard inquiry.

Soft Pull vs Hard Pull (This Is Huge)

Some lenders:

- Use soft inquiries (no score impact)
- Others use hard inquiries (small, temporary impact)

Before requesting an increase:

- Check the issuer's policy
- Ask the rep directly
- Look it up if needed

Always prefer soft-pull increases when possible.

How Often You Can Ask

Most issuers allow:

- Requests every 6–12 months

Asking too often:

- Raises flags
- Leads to denials
- Looks desperate

Patience improves approval odds.

How to Ask (What to Say)

You don't need a speech.

A simple request works:

- "I've been a customer for a while and I'd like to request a credit limit increase."

If asked why:

- Mention on-time payments
- Mention income stability
- Mention responsible use

Do not:

- Mention debt stress
- Mention utilization issues
- Mention hardship

Confidence matters.

How Much to Request

This depends on the issuer, but a good rule:

- Ask for a meaningful increase
- Not something tiny
- Not something outrageous

Many online requests auto-calculate limits. Let the system guide you.

What If You're Denied?

Denial is not punishment.

If denied:

- Ask why
- Note the reason
- Improve that factor
- Try again later

Denials do not hurt your score unless a hard inquiry was involved.

A Warning About Increased Limits

More credit is a tool, not a reward.

Higher limits help only if:

- You don't fill them up
- You don't treat them as spending money

If higher limits lead to higher balances, utilization doesn't improve—it stays the same or gets worse.

Which Cards to Target First

Prioritize:

- Cards with high utilization
- Cards with long histories
- Cards from issuers known for soft pulls

One increase on the right card can move your score more than three increases on low-balance cards.

The Takeaway

Requesting credit limit increases strategically is one of the easiest ways to improve utilization and boost your score without paying down debt. When timed correctly and used responsibly, it's a quiet but powerful move.

In the next section, we'll talk about timing your payments for maximum score impact—the final piece of the utilization puzzle that most people never learn but almost everyone benefits from.

8.5 Timing Your Payments for Maximum Score Impact

This is the part of credit scoring that feels unfair until you understand it—then it feels like a cheat code.

You can pay every bill on time. You can pay in full every month. You can do everything "right"... and still sabotage your score if your timing is off. After 20 years in this field, I can tell you this is one of the biggest reasons people get stuck wondering why their score won't move.

Credit scores don't care that you paid. They care when your balance was reported.

Let's fix that.

The Two Dates That Actually Matter

Every credit card has two important dates:

- Statement closing date
- Payment due date

Most people only pay attention to the due date. That's a mistake.

The statement closing date determines what balance gets reported to the credit bureaus

The due date determines whether you're late

You can pay on time and still report a high balance. That's where scores get hurt.

What Credit Bureaus Actually See

Credit bureaus typically see:

- The balance on your statement closing date
- Not your balance after you pay later

So if your card:

- Closes on the 20th
- Is due on the 15th of the next month

And you:

- Let a high balance sit until the 15th
- Pay in full on the due date

Your report still shows the high balance from the 20th.

From the scoring model's perspective, you're heavily utilizing credit—even if you paid it off later.

The Single Best Timing Strategy

Here it is, plain and simple:

- Pay your card down before the statement closing date.

That's it.

Even a partial payment that lowers the balance before closing can:

- Drop utilization
- Improve your score
- Show up within one reporting cycle

This is why people see sudden score jumps without paying off debt entirely.

How Much Should Be Reported?

For maximum score impact, aim for:

- 1%–5% utilization on one card
- Near-zero balances on others

This shows:

- Active use
- Low risk
- Controlled behavior

Zero across all cards isn't always optimal. One small balance usually scores better.

The "Two-Payment" Method (Very Effective)

For people who use cards regularly, this works well:

- Make an early payment before the statement closes to reduce the balance

Pay the remaining balance by the due date

This lets you:

- Use your card normally
- Avoid high reported utilization
- Stay interest-free

It's boring. It works.

Timing Large Purchases Without Damage

Big expenses happen. The trick is when they happen.

Best approach:

- Make large purchases right after the statement closes
- Pay them down before the next closing date

Worst approach:

- Large purchase right before closing
- Letting it report at high utilization

Same purchase. Completely different score impact.

Why Autopay Alone Isn't Enough

Autopay is great—for avoiding late payments.

But autopay usually:

- Pays on the due date
- After the statement has closed

That protects payment history but does nothing for utilization.

Autopay should be your safety net, not your entire strategy.

How Often Scores Respond to Timing Changes

Utilization has no memory.

That means:

- Changes can reflect in 30–45 days
- Sometimes sooner
- No waiting years for forgiveness

This is why timing is one of the fastest ways to influence your score.

A Common Mistake That Undoes Everything

People learn this strategy, use it once, see a score bump... then stop paying attention.

Utilization resets every month.

If timing slips:

- Balances creep up
- Scores drift down
- Confusion returns

This isn't a one-time hack. It's a habit.

How to Find Your Statement Closing Dates

Check:

- Your online account
- Monthly statements
- Customer service chat

Once you know the date, set:

- Calendar reminders
- Early payment alerts
- Automation where possible

Awareness is most of the battle.

The Takeaway

Timing your payments isn't about tricking the system—it's about understanding what the system measures. When you control when balances are reported, you control one of the fastest-moving parts of your credit score.

That wraps up credit utilization. In the next chapter, we'll shift into building positive credit history—how to add strong, healthy accounts that push your score higher even after the negatives are gone.

Chapter 9: Building Positive Credit History

After removing errors and paying down debt, you might think you're done. Nope. Removing negative items is like cleaning up a messy room - necessary, but you still need to put nice furniture in there. I learned this when my score plateaued at 680. All my negative items were gone, my utilization was perfect, but I still couldn't break into the excellent range because I didn't have enough positive credit history. It felt unfair, like being told I needed five years of experience for an entry-level job. But there are actually legitimate shortcuts here - ways to build positive history fast without waiting years or going into debt. Some of them felt like cheating. They're not. They're just using the credit system's own rules in your favor for once.

This chapter outlines strategies for establishing and strengthening positive credit history, which comprises fifteen percent of your credit score through length of credit history and ten percent through credit mix. You will learn how becoming an authorized user on someone else's established account can immediately add years of positive history to your report. We will examine secured credit cards as controlled-risk tools for building credit when traditional cards are unavailable. This chapter explains credit builder loans, specialized products designed specifically for credit establishment. You will understand the importance of maintaining perfect payment history going forward and how to diversify your credit mix responsibly by incorporating different types of credit accounts without overextending yourself financially or creating unnecessary debt.

9.1 Becoming an Authorized User on Established Accounts

If credit building were a video game, becoming an authorized user would feel like finding a hidden shortcut the designers forgot to remove. It's one of the fastest ways to add positive history to your credit report without taking on new debt—and yes, it's completely legal when done correctly.

After 20 years in this field, I can tell you this strategy has helped people jump scores in months instead of years. It has also gone wrong when done carelessly. The difference comes down to who you choose, which account you use, and how well you understand the rules.

Let's break it down.

What Being an Authorized User Actually Means

When you're added as an authorized user:

- You're added to someone else's credit card account
- The account's history can appear on your credit report
- You're not legally responsible for the debt
- You don't need to use the card at all

You're essentially borrowing their good credit behavior.

Why This Works So Well

Authorized user accounts can add:

- Years of positive payment history
- A higher credit limit

- Lower utilization
- An older average age of accounts

All of those factors strengthen your credit profile at once.

That's why this strategy can move scores quickly.

The Ideal Authorized User Account

Not all accounts help equally.

The best authorized user accounts have:

- Long account history (the older, the better)
- Perfect payment history
- Low utilization (ideally under 10%)
- No late payments
- A reputable major card issuer

One great account beats three mediocre ones.

Who Should Add You (This Matters)

This should be:

- Someone you trust completely
- Someone financially responsible
- Someone who doesn't carry high balances
- Someone unlikely to miss payments

Family members are common, but trust matters more than blood.

If they mess up, your credit gets hit too.

You Do NOT Need the Card

Let me repeat this clearly: you do not need access to the card.

In most cases:

- Don't take the card
- Don't use the card
- Don't attach it to any spending apps

This strategy is about reporting—not spending.

How Fast Results Show Up

Typically:

- The account reports within 1–2 billing cycles
- Score impact can appear within 30–60 days
- Older, cleaner accounts show results faster

This is one of the quickest positive changes you can make.

When Authorized User Status Helps Most

This strategy is especially effective if:

- Your credit file is thin
- Your accounts are new
- You're rebuilding after damage
- You lack long credit history

It's less impactful if you already have a thick, established file.

Risks People Don't Think About

There are real risks if you choose poorly.

Potential downsides:

- The primary user runs up balances
- Payments are missed
- The account gets closed
- Utilization spikes unexpectedly

Any of these can drag your score down.

Monitor the account like it's yours—because functionally, it is.

Should You Use Authorized User Tradelines for a Fee?

This is where things get tricky.

Paid tradeline services exist, but:

- Some issuers ignore them
- Some scoring models discount them
- They can be expensive
- Results aren't guaranteed

Natural authorized user relationships are safer and more reliable.

How Many Authorized User Accounts Do You Need?

Usually:

- One or two strong accounts is plenty
- More is not better
- Quality beats quantity

Overdoing it can look artificial.

How to Remove Yourself If Needed

If something changes:

- Ask to be removed immediately
- Removal usually updates reports quickly
- Damage stops once removed

This is a reversible strategy—which is a big plus.

The Takeaway

Becoming an authorized user on a well-managed account can add years of positive history almost overnight. When done carefully, it's one of the smartest shortcuts in credit building. When done carelessly, it can backfire just as fast.

In the next section, we'll talk about secured credit cards—how to use them as rebuilding tools without falling into unnecessary fees or bad products.

9.2 Secured Credit Cards as a Rebuilding Tool

Secured credit cards don't get much love. People hear "secured" and think, "Great, I have to give them my own money just to borrow it back." I get the skepticism. I had it too. But after 20 years in this field, I can tell you this: used correctly, secured cards are one of the safest and most effective ways to rebuild credit from the ground up.

Used incorrectly, they're just expensive training wheels you never take off.

Let's make sure you're in the first group.

What a Secured Credit Card Actually Is

A secured credit card requires:

- A refundable cash deposit
- That deposit becomes your credit limit

Example:

$500 deposit = $500 credit limit

From a reporting standpoint, it behaves just like a regular credit card:

- Payments are reported monthly
- Utilization matters
- Payment history counts

The difference is the risk—yours, not theirs.

Why Secured Cards Are Great for Rebuilding

Secured cards work because they:

- Are easier to get approved for
- Limit overspending by design
- Allow controlled utilization
- Build positive payment history

For people rebuilding after mistakes, this structure is a feature, not a flaw.

Who Should Use a Secured Card

Secured cards are ideal if:

- You have little or no credit history
- You're rebuilding after delinquencies or collections
- You've been denied for unsecured cards
- You want a low-risk way to add positive history

If you already qualify for good unsecured cards, secured cards may not add much value.

What to Look for in a Good Secured Card

Not all secured cards are created equal.

Look for:

- Reporting to all three credit bureaus
- Reasonable deposit requirements
- No hidden fees
- Clear upgrade path to unsecured

- Reputable issuer

Avoid cards that:

- Charge excessive monthly fees
- Don't report regularly
- Make it hard to graduate

The goal is rebuilding—not paying fees forever.

How Much Should You Deposit?

Deposit:

- Only what you can comfortably afford
- Enough to keep utilization low

A $300–$500 limit is usually plenty.

You don't need a huge limit—you need good behavior.

How to Use a Secured Card Correctly

Best practices:

- Use it lightly
- Keep utilization under 10%
- Pay before the statement closes
- Pay in full every month

Treat it like a credit-building tool, not spending money.

How Fast Secured Cards Help

Typically:

- Reporting begins within 30 days
- Positive history builds immediately
- Score improvements show within a few months

They don't create miracles—but they create momentum.

When to Upgrade or Move On

Many secured cards:

- Automatically review accounts after 6–12 months
- Offer conversion to unsecured
- Return your deposit upon upgrade

If yours doesn't:

- Ask
- Or plan to move on after solid history is built

Secured cards are a phase, not a permanent solution.

A Common Mistake That Ruins the Benefit

People max out secured cards thinking:

- "It's my money anyway."

From a scoring standpoint, it doesn't matter whose money it is. High utilization still hurts.

Low balances win.

Secured Cards vs Authorized User Accounts

They serve different roles:

- **Authorized user** = borrowed history
- **Secured card** = your own behavior

Used together, they're powerful.

The Takeaway

Secured credit cards are not a step backward—they're a controlled step forward. When used strategically, they build real, lasting credit without the risk of spiraling debt.

In the next section, we'll talk about credit builder loans—another specialized tool that can help add positive history when used the right way.

9.3 Credit Builder Loans and How They Work

Credit builder loans sound backwards the first time you hear about them. You take out a loan, but you don't get the money. You make payments, and then you get the money later. It feels like a financial prank.

I thought the same thing the first time I saw one. After 20 years in this field, though, I can tell you this: credit builder loans are not about the cash—they're about creating the right kind of credit history. When used correctly, they're a solid tool for people who need installment credit on their reports without taking on real risk.

Let's unpack how they actually work and when they're worth using.

What a Credit Builder Loan Is

A credit builder loan is a small installment loan designed specifically to build credit.

Here's the basic structure:

- You "borrow" a small amount (usually $300–$1,500)
- The money is placed in a locked savings account
- You make monthly payments over a set term
- Payments are reported to credit bureaus
- When the loan is paid off, you get the money

From the credit system's perspective, you successfully repaid an installment loan. That's the entire point.

Why Credit Builder Loans Exist

Many people rebuilding credit have:

- Credit cards only
- Or no active credit at all

Credit builder loans add:

- Installment credit
- On-time payment history
- Credit mix diversity

They help fill a specific gap.

Who Benefits Most from Credit Builder Loans

These loans make sense if:

- You have a thin credit file
- You lack installment accounts
- You're rebuilding after major negatives
- You want structured, low-risk credit building

They're less useful if you already have multiple installment loans reporting.

How Credit Builder Loans Affect Your Credit

They impact:

- Payment history (positively, if paid on time)
- Credit mix
- Account age over time

They don't affect utilization the same way cards do, but they still strengthen your profile.

Consistency matters more than speed here.

How Long the Loan Should Be

Most credit builder loans range from:

- 6 months
- 12 months
- 24 months

Longer terms:

- Build history over time
- Cost slightly more in fees

Shorter terms:

- Build faster
- End sooner

There's no perfect term—just avoid anything excessively long.

What to Watch Out For

Not all credit builder loans are consumer-friendly.

Avoid loans with:

- High fees
- Excessive interest
- Poor reporting practices

- No clear savings release

The cost should be minimal. You're paying for reporting—not borrowing.

How to Use a Credit Builder Loan Correctly

Best practices:

- Set autopay
- Never miss a payment
- Treat it as non-negotiable
- Let it run its course

Missed payments defeat the purpose completely.

Credit Builder Loans vs Secured Cards

They serve different roles:

- **Secured card** = revolving credit behavior
- **Credit builder loan** = installment credit behavior

Used together, they create balance.

You don't need both, but many people benefit from the combination.

A Common Misunderstanding

People expect instant score jumps.

Credit builder loans are:

- Slow and steady
- History-focused
- Long-term builders

They don't spike scores overnight—but they help raise ceilings over time.

When to Close the Loan

When the loan is paid off:

- History remains
- On-time payments stay
- Credit mix remains positive

You don't need to repeat endlessly. One or two well-managed loans are enough.

The Takeaway

Credit builder loans are boring—and that's why they work. They quietly add positive installment history without risking debt spirals. Used intentionally, they're a reliable tool for strengthening your credit foundation.

In the next section, we'll talk about maintaining perfect payment history going forward—because once positive credit is built, protecting it is just as important as creating it.

9.4 Maintaining Perfect Payment History Going Forward

Payment history is the heavyweight champion of your credit score. It makes up the largest portion of your score, and unlike utilization, it has a long memory. Missed payments stick around for years, and one careless mistake can undo months of progress.

After 20 years in this field, I can tell you something reassuring, though: maintaining perfect payment history is far easier than repairing bad payment history—if you build the right systems.

This section isn't about willpower. It's about removing opportunities to mess up.

Why Payment History Matters So Much

Payment history answers one core question:

- "Does this person pay what they owe, when they owe it?"

Late payments signal:

- Financial instability
- Disorganization
- Higher default risk

Even one 30-day late payment can:

- Drop scores significantly
- Affect approvals
- Stay on your report for seven years

That's why prevention matters more than correction.

The Myth of "I'll Remember"

You won't. Nobody does.

Life gets busy. Bills stack up. Due dates shift. That's not a character flaw—it's reality. Relying on memory is how perfect histories get ruined.

Automation beats intention every time.

The Non-Negotiable Rule: Autopay Minimums

Every single account you have should have:

- Autopay set for at least the minimum payment

Even if you plan to pay more manually, autopay is your safety net.

If you do nothing else after reading this chapter, do this.

Align Due Dates to Reduce Friction

Many lenders allow you to:

- Change due dates
- Align them across accounts

Having:

- 10 different due dates

is much harder than:

- 1 or 2 predictable windows

Fewer dates = fewer mistakes.

Use Alerts as Backup, Not Primary Defense

Set:

- Payment reminders
- Balance alerts
- Statement notifications

But remember:

- Alerts can be missed
- Phones die
- Emails go unread

Autopay is primary. Alerts are backup.

Keep a Small Cash Buffer (This Is Credit Protection)

A missed payment often isn't about irresponsibility—it's about timing.

A small buffer:

- Prevents overdrafts
- Covers minimums during tight months
- Stops emergencies from becoming credit disasters

Even $500 can protect thousands of points over time.

Watch Out for "Set It and Forget It" Traps

Autopay only works if:

- The linked account has money
- Cards don't change terms
- Accounts don't get closed or replaced

Check autopay quarterly. Five minutes. Worth it.

Handle Hard Months Strategically

If money gets tight:

- Prioritize minimum payments
- Call creditors early
- Ask for hardship options
- Avoid skipping payments silently

Many lenders offer:

- Temporary deferrals
- Fee waivers
- Payment adjustments

Late payments happen when communication doesn't.

One Late Payment Is Not a Moral Failure

Let's be clear.

If you mess up:

- Don't panic
- Don't ignore it
- Don't assume it's permanent

Sometimes:

- Fees can be reversed
- Lates can be corrected (especially first-time)

- Damage can be minimized

Address issues immediately.

Why Perfect Payment History Gets Easier Over Time

As you progress:

- Debt decreases
- Cash flow improves
- Systems stabilize
- Stress drops

Credit maintenance becomes boring—and boring is good.

A Quiet Benefit Nobody Mentions

Perfect payment history:

- Improves negotiation leverage
- Helps with rate reductions
- Strengthens lender relationships
- Opens doors beyond the score

It's not just about numbers—it's about options.

The Takeaway

Perfect payment history isn't about discipline—it's about design. When you remove friction and automate protection, paying on time becomes the default, not a daily decision.

In the next section, we'll talk about diversifying your credit mix responsibly—how to add the right kinds of accounts without overextending or undoing your progress.

9.5 Diversifying Your Credit Mix Responsibly

At some point in rebuilding credit, people hit a weird plateau. Payments are perfect. Utilization is low. Negatives are aging or gone. And yet... the score just sits there. This is usually when credit mix enters the conversation.

Credit mix matters—but not nearly as much as the internet makes it sound. After 20 years in this field, I can tell you this clearly: credit mix helps polish a strong profile; it does not rescue a weak one. Used responsibly, it can push scores higher. Used recklessly, it creates new problems for no good reason.

Let's talk about how to do this the smart way.

What Credit Mix Actually Means

Credit mix refers to the types of credit on your report, not how many accounts you have.

Broadly, credit falls into two categories:

- Revolving credit (credit cards, lines of credit)
- Installment credit (auto loans, personal loans, student loans, mortgages)

Scoring models like to see that you can manage both.

How Much Credit Mix Really Matters

Credit mix typically accounts for about 10% of your score.

That means:

- It matters

- But it's not worth wrecking your finances over

If payment history and utilization aren't solid, credit mix won't save you. Think of it as seasoning, not the main dish.

What a "Healthy" Credit Mix Looks Like

For most people, an ideal mix is:

- One to three revolving accounts
- One installment account (current or past)

That's it.

You do not need:

- A car loan if you don't need a car
- A personal loan just to "add variety"

Five different account types to impress the algorithm

Simplicity wins.

The Biggest Credit Mix Mistake People Make

Opening unnecessary debt.

I've seen people:

- Take out loans they didn't need
- Pay interest for no reason
- Create payment risk
- All for a few theoretical points

That's backwards.

Never take on debt only for credit mix unless the risk is extremely controlled.

Responsible Ways to Improve Credit Mix

If your profile is card-heavy and stable, these can make sense:

Credit builder loans

- Low risk, structured, purpose-built for this exact need

Existing installment loans

- Even closed, paid-off installment loans still contribute positively to mix and history

Authorized user accounts

- While still revolving, they strengthen depth without new risk

You don't need to add everything—just enough balance.

When to Add Installment Credit

Consider adding installment credit only if:

- Your revolving credit is under control
- Payments are automated and reliable
- You can afford it comfortably
- There's a real benefit beyond scoring

If adding an installment loan causes stress, it's not responsible diversification.

When NOT to Worry About Credit Mix

Don't focus on credit mix if:

- You're still missing payments

- Utilization is high
- Collections are unresolved
- Cash flow is tight

Fix fundamentals first. Mix comes later.

Why Closed Accounts Still Help You

This is good news.

Paid-off installment loans:

- Remain on your report
- Continue contributing to mix
- Support length of credit history

You don't need to keep loans open forever to get the benefit.

A Quiet Truth About Excellent Credit

People with excellent credit often:

- Have boring credit profiles
- Don't open accounts often
- Avoid unnecessary complexity

Their mix looks good because time did the work—not because they chased points.

How to Think About Credit Mix Going Forward

Ask one simple question before adding anything new:

- "Does this improve my financial life and my credit?"

- If the answer is only credit, pause.
- If the answer is both, proceed carefully.

The Takeaway

Diversifying your credit mix responsibly is about balance, not accumulation. One well-managed installment account combined with clean revolving credit is usually enough to unlock higher score ranges without adding unnecessary risk.

That completes building positive credit history. In the next chapter, we'll move into rebuilding after bankruptcy or foreclosure—how to recover from major setbacks faster and smarter than most people think is possible.

Chapter 10: Rebuilding After Bankruptcy or Foreclosure

Bankruptcy. Foreclosure. Even writing these words probably makes your stomach drop. These are the nuclear options, the financial disasters we're told we'll never recover from. When my cousin filed Chapter 7, family members acted like he'd committed a crime. "His credit is ruined forever," they whispered. Except here's the truth nobody mentions: bankruptcy and foreclosure are temporary. Yes, they hurt. Yes, they stay on your report for seven to ten years. But they don't have to control your financial life for that entire time. I've watched people recover from bankruptcy and hit 700 credit scores within two years. Not by doing anything illegal or sketchy, just by understanding that these major negative items lose their power over time and knowing exactly how to build positive history that outweighs them. Your financial life isn't over. It's just on hard mode for a while.

This chapter addresses credit rebuilding strategies following major financial setbacks including Chapter 7 and Chapter 13 bankruptcy, foreclosure, short sale, and repossession. You will learn the specific timeframes these items remain on your credit report and how their impact diminishes over time. We will examine how to rebuild credit during and immediately after Chapter 7 bankruptcy liquidation versus the different approach required during Chapter 13 repayment plans. This chapter provides recovery timelines and strategies specific to foreclosure and short sale situations. You will receive a comprehensive twelve-month action plan that outlines specific steps to take each month following a major negative event, including when to apply for new credit, how to explain past issues to potential creditors, and realistic score improvement expectations based on starting points and consistent effort.

10.1 Understanding How Long Negative Items Remain on Your Report

One of the biggest sources of fear around credit is the belief that mistakes last forever. I hear this constantly: "I ruined my credit years ago, so what's the point?" After 20 years in this field, let me clear this up right now: credit damage is temporary, even when it feels permanent.

Negative items have expiration dates. The problem is that most people don't know which dates matter, which don't, and how reporting timelines actually work. That confusion keeps people stuck longer than necessary.

Let's put some structure around this.

The Golden Rule of Credit Reporting Timelines

Most negative information stays on your credit report for about seven years. Not from when the account was paid. Not from when it was sold. Not from the last time a collector contacted you.

It's based on the Date of First Delinquency—the moment you first missed a payment and never brought the account current again.

That date controls almost everything.

Why the Date of First Delinquency Is So Important

This date:

- Starts the reporting clock
- Determines when the account must fall off
- Cannot legally be reset by payment or sale

If this date is wrong, an account can stay on your report longer than allowed. That's not bad luck—that's a dispute opportunity.

Common Negative Items and Their Reporting Limits

Here's what you'll typically see:

- **Late payments:** 7 years
- **Collections:** 7 years from the original account's delinquency
- **Charge-offs:** 7 years
- **Repossessions:** 7 years
- **Foreclosures:** 7 years
- **Chapter 13 bankruptcy:** 7 years from filing
- **Chapter 7 bankruptcy:** 10 years from filing

If something is still reporting beyond these limits, it doesn't belong there.

Paid vs Unpaid Does Not Change the Clock

This surprises people.

Paying a debt:

- Does not reset reporting time
- Does not extend how long it stays
- Does not "restart" the seven years

Time is tied to delinquency, not resolution.

This is why you should never rush to pay an old debt without understanding the timeline first.

Why Old Negatives Hurt Less Over Time

Credit scoring models weigh recency heavily.

That means:

- A late payment from last month hurts far more than one from five years ago
- Old collections have diminishing impact
- Time quietly works in your favor

This is why people can rebuild strong scores even while old negatives still technically exist.

Why Some Accounts Seem to Never Go Away

This usually happens because of:

- Incorrect delinquency dates
- Re-aging by collectors
- Mixed or duplicated files
- Reporting errors

Negative items don't "stick around forever" legally—but they do sometimes linger improperly.

That's why reviewing dates matters.

The Difference Between Reporting Time and Legal Time

This is critical and often misunderstood.

- Credit reporting time controls how long something appears on your report
- Statute of limitations controls how long you can be sued

They are not the same thing. A debt can fall off your credit report but still technically exist, or be time-barred legally but still reportable for a while.

Different clocks. Different rules.

Why Waiting Alone Is Not a Strategy

Yes, time helps—but passive waiting wastes opportunity.

Smart rebuilding involves:

- Removing errors early
- Building positive history in parallel
- Letting old damage fade naturally

You don't have to choose between action and patience. You use both.

A Common Psychological Trap

People fixate on the removal date and do nothing until then.

That's a mistake.

By the time a negative item falls off:

- Your score can already be strong
- Lenders can already say yes
- The past can already be outweighed

Credit improvement is cumulative, not sequential.

How to Check Removal Dates Correctly

Look for:

- Date of first delinquency

- Estimated removal date
- Account status history

If dates don't align across bureaus, that's a red flag worth investigating.

The Takeaway

Negative credit items are not life sentences. They are time-bound data points that lose power every year—especially when you build positive history alongside them. Once you understand how long things last and why, fear turns into strategy.

In the next section, we'll dig into rebuilding credit during and after Chapter 7 bankruptcy—how to work with the timeline instead of being crushed by it.

10.2 Rebuilding Credit During and After Chapter 7 Bankruptcy

Chapter 7 bankruptcy gets talked about like it's the end of your financial life. Like once it's on your report, the doors close, the lights go off, and you're stuck in credit purgatory for ten years. That's dramatic—and wrong.

After 20 years in this field, I've watched people file Chapter 7, follow a smart rebuilding plan, and be back in the high 600s or low 700s within two years. Not through tricks. Not through shady shortcuts. Through understanding how bankruptcy actually works in the credit system and using that knowledge instead of fighting it.

Let's talk about how to rebuild the right way.

First: What Chapter 7 Really Does to Your Credit

Chapter 7 is a liquidation bankruptcy. Most unsecured debts are wiped out, and the case stays on your credit report for up to 10 years from the filing date.

That sounds awful until you understand two key truths:

- The impact of bankruptcy fades much faster than its presence

- Post-bankruptcy behavior matters more than pre-bankruptcy damage

- Your score often drops sharply at first—but then the slate is oddly clean.

Why Credit Can Improve Faster After Bankruptcy

Here's the paradox: bankruptcy can make rebuilding easier than limping along with unresolved debt.

After discharge:

- Old debts show zero balances
- Collections stop updating
- Utilization often drops dramatically
- No more late payments on discharged accounts

You go from "constantly bleeding" to "stabilized."

Stability is rebuildable.

What You Should Do During an Active Chapter 7 Case

While your case is open:

- Do not apply for new credit unless advised
- Focus on cash flow and budgeting
- Set up a small emergency buffer
- Monitor your credit reports for errors

Some lenders offer credit during this phase, but patience usually pays better.

Step One After Discharge: Clean Up Your Reports

Once your bankruptcy is discharged, pull all three credit reports.

You're looking for:

- Accounts that weren't included but should have been
- Discharged debts still showing balances
- Incorrect statuses like "charged off" instead of "included in bankruptcy"

These are common errors—and they're fixable.

Your reports should reflect that those debts are no longer collectible.

Step Two: Re-Establish Credit Carefully

You don't rebuild by opening everything that approves you. You rebuild with control.

Strong early rebuilding tools include:

- One secured credit card
- Possibly a credit builder loan
- Authorized user status on a clean account

You're not trying to look wealthy. You're trying to look stable.

How Many Accounts Do You Actually Need?

Early on:

- One revolving account is enough
- Two is plenty
- More than that is unnecessary

Each new account adds risk. Slow and steady wins here.

How to Use New Credit Post-Bankruptcy

This part matters more than the account itself.

Best practices:

- Keep utilization under 10%
- Pay before the statement closes
- Never miss a payment
- Let accounts age

Post-bankruptcy credit is judged harshly. Perfect behavior is non-negotiable.

When to Expect Real Score Movement

Typical pattern I see:

- **First 3–6 months:** stabilization
- **6–12 months:** noticeable improvement
- **12–24 months:** strong recovery range if behavior is clean

People get discouraged too early. Time plus consistency does the heavy lifting.

Why You Should Ignore "Credit Repair Shortcuts" After Bankruptcy

You'll see ads promising:

- Instant 700 scores
- Bankruptcy removal
- Secret loopholes

None of that is real.

Bankruptcy is accurate information. You don't remove it early. You outweigh it.

Anyone telling you otherwise is selling hope, not strategy.

A Common Post-Bankruptcy Mistake

People treat new credit like a second chance to overspend.

They think:

- "I already filed. What's the worst that could happen?"

That mindset leads right back to trouble.

Post-bankruptcy credit discipline determines whether this was a reset—or a repeat.

The Emotional Side Nobody Talks About

Bankruptcy carries shame for a lot of people. That shame often leads to avoidance, not action.

Here's the truth: lenders care far more about what you do after bankruptcy than why you filed. Life happens. Systems fail. People recover.

Your job now is to demonstrate reliability.

The Takeaway

Chapter 7 bankruptcy is not a financial death sentence—it's a hard reset. When you clean up reporting errors, rebuild slowly, and maintain flawless habits, credit recovery happens faster than most people expect.

In the next section, we'll talk about rebuilding credit during and after Chapter 13 bankruptcy, which follows a very different timeline and requires a different strategy to get the best results.

10.3 Credit Recovery Strategies After Chapter 13 Bankruptcy

Chapter 13 bankruptcy doesn't get as much attention as Chapter 7, but it brings its own unique challenges—and opportunities. Instead of wiping the slate clean quickly, Chapter 13 puts you on a structured repayment plan that can last three to five years. That sounds exhausting, and honestly, it can be. But after 20 years in this field, I can tell you this: people who handle Chapter 13 correctly often come out with stronger long-term credit habits than they ever had before.

The key is understanding that Chapter 13 recovery happens in phases, not all at once.

How Chapter 13 Affects Your Credit Differently

Chapter 13 remains on your credit report for seven years from the filing date, not ten. That alone gives it a slightly shorter shadow than Chapter 7.

More importantly:

- You are actively repaying debts
- Accounts may continue reporting during the plan
- Payment consistency becomes the spotlight

Your behavior during the plan matters a lot.

Phase One: Rebuilding While the Plan Is Active

This is where most people assume rebuilding is impossible. It's not.

During an active Chapter 13 plan:

- Trustee payments are critical

- One missed payment can derail everything
- Budget discipline is non-negotiable

Credit rebuilding here is conservative—but possible.

Credit Options During Chapter 13

Most trustees allow limited new credit with approval.

Common options include:

- A secured credit card
- A small credit builder loan (with approval)
- Occasionally an auto loan if necessary

The goal is not growth—it's proof of consistency.

Always get written trustee approval before opening anything new.

How to Use Credit During the Plan

If approved:

- Keep balances extremely low
- Use the card occasionally
- Pay before the statement closes
- Never miss a payment

Your margin for error during Chapter 13 is very small.

Monitoring Your Credit During the Plan

Pull your reports regularly.

Watch for:

- Accounts incorrectly marked as late
- Discharged or included debts still updating
- Duplicate accounts

Errors during Chapter 13 are common—and damaging if ignored.

Phase Two: The Final Year of the Plan

The final year is crucial.

This is when you:

- Maintain perfect trustee payments
- Avoid opening new accounts
- Prepare for post-discharge rebuilding

Think of this phase as stabilization before acceleration.

Phase Three: After Chapter 13 Discharge

Once the plan is completed and discharged:

- Remaining eligible debts are cleared
- Your risk profile improves immediately
- Lenders start to look at you differently

This is when rebuilding can accelerate.

Post-Discharge Rebuilding Strategy

After discharge, focus on:

- One or two revolving accounts
- Low utilization

- Perfect payment history
- Gradual account aging

You don't need to rush. Time is now on your side.

Why Chapter 13 Can Lead to Stronger Credit Long-Term

People who complete Chapter 13 often:

- Develop strong budgeting habits
- Understand cash flow better
- Respect credit limits
- Avoid impulsive borrowing

Those habits outlast the bankruptcy notation.

A Common Chapter 13 Mistake

- People get impatient near the end and overextend too soon.
- Finishing strong matters more than starting fast.
- Wait for discharge. Then move strategically.

The Emotional Reality of Chapter 13

Chapter 13 requires endurance. It's a marathon, not a sprint. The frustration is real—but so is the payoff.

Completing the plan proves reliability in a way few things do.

The Takeaway

Chapter 13 recovery is slower, but it's structured. When you respect the process, protect your payments, and rebuild carefully at each phase, you don't just recover—you emerge more stable than before.

In the next section, we'll cover recovering from foreclosure or short sale—another major setback that feels permanent but fades faster than most people expect when handled correctly.

10.4 Recovering from Foreclosure or Short Sale

Foreclosure and short sale are two of the most emotionally loaded events in personal finance. They're not just credit events—they're life events. People don't talk about them openly, but after 20 years in this field, I've seen the same pattern over and over: the emotional damage lasts longer than the credit damage.

The good news is this—foreclosure and short sale feel permanent, but in the credit system, they are not. They follow clear timelines, their impact fades, and with the right strategy, recovery happens faster than most people expect.

Let's walk through how this actually works.

Foreclosure vs Short Sale: What's the Difference?

From a credit perspective:

- Foreclosure happens when the lender takes the property after default
- Short sale occurs when the home is sold for less than the amount owed with lender approval

Both are serious negative events, but neither ends your financial future.

Short sales are generally viewed slightly more favorably than foreclosures—but both follow similar recovery paths.

How Long These Events Stay on Your Credit Report

Both foreclosure and short sale typically remain on your credit report for seven years from the date of first delinquency related to the mortgage.

That timeline:

- Cannot be reset
- Does not change if the property is later sold
- Applies regardless of deficiency balances

Time is fixed. Impact is not.

Why the Damage Feels Worse Than It Is

Mortgage-related negatives hurt more because:

- Mortgages are large loans
- Housing is tied to identity and stability
- The event is highly visible to lenders

But here's the key: scoring models focus on recent behavior more than past disasters.

Your score can begin recovering long before the seven years are up.

The First Step: Stabilize Housing and Cash Flow

Before worrying about credit:

- Secure stable housing
- Lock in affordable payments
- Rebuild an emergency buffer

Credit rebuilding fails when life is unstable.

Stability comes first.

Cleaning Up Credit Reports After Foreclosure or Short Sale

Pull all three reports and check:

- Correct delinquency dates
- Accurate status (foreclosure vs settled)
- No duplicate mortgage accounts
- No re-aging of late payments

Mortgage reporting errors are common and worth disputing.

When to Start Rebuilding Credit

You don't need to wait years.

Once the foreclosure or short sale is complete:

- New positive credit can be added
- Utilization and payment history can improve
- Scores can start rising within months

Waiting does not help more than building.

Smart Rebuilding Tools After Housing Loss

Effective early tools include:

- One secured credit card
- Authorized user status on a clean account
- Careful installment credit if needed

The goal is consistency, not speed.

How Long Until You Can Buy Again?

This depends on:

- Loan type

- Down payment
- Credit rebuilding efforts

Many people qualify for:

- FHA loans in 2–3 years
- Conventional loans in 4–7 years

Rebuilding early shortens these timelines.

Why Lenders Care More About the Recovery Than the Event

Lenders ask:

- Did the person learn?
- Are finances stable now?
- Is there a pattern of responsibility post-event?

A clean recovery story often matters more than the initial setback.

A Common Recovery Mistake

Avoid this mindset:

- "I already lost a house, so credit doesn't matter."

That thinking delays recovery more than the foreclosure itself.

Your next opportunity depends on what you do after—not what happened before.

The Emotional Side (Because It Matters)

Foreclosure and short sale often involve:

- Shame

- Grief
- Loss of identity
- Avoidance

Those emotions are real—but they don't belong on your credit report forever.

Separating emotion from strategy is a turning point.

The Takeaway

Foreclosure and short sale are painful chapters, not permanent labels. With stable housing, clean reporting, and steady rebuilding, their impact fades faster than most people believe.

In the next section, we'll pull everything together with a 12-month credit rebuilding action plan—a step-by-step roadmap for moving forward after major financial setbacks.

10.5 Creating a 12-Month Credit Rebuilding Action Plan

When people ask me how long credit rebuilding takes, my honest answer after 20 years is: it depends on what you do in the first 12 months. That first year sets the tone for everything that follows. Not because magic happens in month twelve, but because habits, systems, and momentum are established early.

This plan isn't about perfection. It's about consistent, boring progress. That's what actually works.

Think of this as a roadmap, not a prison sentence. Adjust as needed, but don't ignore it.

Months 1–3: Stabilize and Clean Up

This phase is about stopping the bleeding and creating a clean foundation.

Your priorities:

- Pull all three credit reports
- Review every account for accuracy
- Dispute obvious errors and outdated information
- Confirm delinquency dates are correct
- Set autopay on every active account
- Build a small emergency buffer (even $500 helps)

Do not apply for new credit yet unless rebuilding tools are necessary and intentional.

The goal here is control, not growth.

Months 4–6: Establish Positive Activity

Now that things are stable, it's time to add controlled, positive behavior.

What this phase looks like:

- Open one secured credit card if needed
- Consider authorized user status on a clean account
- Keep utilization under 10%
- Pay before statement closing dates
- Never miss a payment

This is where consistency starts showing up in your reports.

Expect modest score movement—not fireworks yet.

Months 7–9: Build Momentum and Optimize

This is where many people get impatient. Don't.

Your job now is to optimize, not expand recklessly.

Focus areas:

- Request credit limit increases (soft pull preferred)
- Continue reducing utilization
- Add a credit builder loan only if it truly helps your mix
- Monitor reports monthly
- Address lingering inaccuracies

You should start seeing noticeable score improvements here if behavior is clean.

Months 10–12: Prepare for the Next Level

This phase is about positioning yourself for better opportunities.

What to do:

- Review progress against goals
- Avoid unnecessary new accounts
- Let accounts age
- Maintain perfect payment history
- Keep balances low and predictable

At this point, lenders are starting to see a pattern—not just recovery, but reliability.

What Not to Do During the 12 Months

Avoid these common mistakes:

- Opening multiple accounts quickly
- Chasing every approval
- Ignoring utilization because "payments are on time"
- Closing old accounts unnecessarily
- Giving up after one slow month

Credit rebuilding punishes impatience more than mistakes.

What Real Success Looks Like After 12 Months

Success is not just a number.

It looks like:

- Predictable bills

- Automated payments
- Lower stress
- Fewer surprises

A credit profile that improves without micromanagement

The score follows the system—not the other way around.

Why This Plan Works

This plan works because:

- It respects how credit scoring actually functions
- It builds habits before chasing results
- It balances patience with action
- It assumes you're human

Credit recovery is not about fixing the past. It's about proving the future is different.

The Takeaway

A 12-month rebuilding plan isn't about rushing—it's about stacking small wins until they compound. When you stabilize first, build second, and optimize last, credit recovery stops feeling overwhelming and starts feeling inevitable.

That completes rebuilding after major setbacks. In the next chapter, we'll shift into maintaining and protecting your credit long-term—how to keep the progress you've earned and make sure you never have to rebuild from scratch again.

Chapter 11: Maintaining and Protecting Your Credit Long-Term

So you've done it. You've disputed errors, paid down debt, rebuilt your score, and finally achieved that excellent credit rating you've been chasing. Congratulations. Now don't screw it up. I'm serious. I worked my score up to 780, got cocky, stopped monitoring my credit, and didn't notice when a gym I'd canceled kept charging a card I'd forgotten about. Those missed payments cost me sixty points before I even realized what happened. Good credit isn't a destination where you plant a flag and declare victory. It's more like a garden that needs regular attention or else weeds start growing. The good news? Maintaining excellent credit is way easier than building it in the first place. You just need systems in place so you never accidentally fall back into old patterns or miss warning signs of problems developing.

This chapter focuses on long-term credit management strategies and protection mechanisms that preserve your improved credit score indefinitely. You will learn to implement credit monitoring systems that alert you to changes, new accounts, or suspicious activity in real-time, enabling rapid response to identity theft or reporting errors. We will develop an annual credit report review checklist that ensures you catch and correct issues before they become serious problems. This chapter covers comprehensive identity theft protection strategies, from freezing your credit reports to monitoring the dark web for compromised personal information. You will establish daily and monthly credit habits that maintain high scores without requiring constant attention or anxiety. Finally, we will discuss passing financial literacy to the next generation, ensuring your children or dependents learn these lessons earlier than you did, breaking cycles of credit problems before they begin.

11.1 Setting Up Credit Monitoring and Alerts

Rebuilding your credit is hard. Protecting it is much easier—if you actually know when something changes. The problem is most people don't. They assume no news is good news, and after 20 years in this field, I can tell you that assumption costs people points they never saw coming.

Credit monitoring isn't about obsession. It's about early detection. Catching problems when they're small instead of discovering them six months later when the damage is already done.

Let's set this up the smart way.

What Credit Monitoring Actually Does

Credit monitoring:

- Alerts you to changes on your credit report
- Notifies you of new accounts, inquiries, or balance changes
- Helps catch errors and fraud early
- Gives you visibility instead of surprise

It does not:

- Prevent identity theft
- Fix errors automatically
- Replace reviewing your reports

Think of it as a smoke detector, not a fire extinguisher.

Why Monitoring Matters More After Rebuilding

When your credit is poor, changes don't move the needle much. When your credit is good, small changes matter a lot.

After rebuilding:

- One missed payment can drop you 50+ points
- One fraudulent account can wreck approvals
- One reporting error can stall progress

Monitoring protects momentum.

Free vs Paid Monitoring (The Honest Take)

You don't need expensive monitoring to stay protected.

Free monitoring usually includes:

- Alerts for major changes
- Access to one bureau
- Basic score tracking

Paid monitoring may add:

- All three bureaus
- More frequent updates
- Identity theft insurance
- Dark web scans

For most people, free or low-cost monitoring is enough—especially if paired with regular report reviews.

What Alerts You Actually Need

Not all alerts are useful. Focus on these:

- New accounts opened
- New hard inquiries
- Missed or late payments
- Balance increases
- Address or name changes

Ignore the noise about minor score fluctuations.

How Often You Should Check Your Credit

Alerts: real-time or near real-time

- **Reports:** at least once per year per bureau
- **Scores:** monthly is plenty

Daily checking adds stress without adding insight.

Set Alerts Where You Already Look

The best alert system is one you'll actually notice.

Use:

- Email notifications you check
- App notifications you don't mute
- Text alerts if available

A perfect system you ignore is useless.

Monitoring Alone Is Not Enough

Monitoring only works if you act.

If you get an alert:

- Review it immediately
- Confirm it's accurate
- Dispute errors quickly
- Freeze credit if fraud is suspected

Speed limits damage.

A Common Monitoring Mistake

People confuse monitoring with management.

- Monitoring tells you something changed.
- Management is what you do next.

Never assume "they'll fix it."

When to Consider Credit Freezes

If:

- You're not applying for credit soon
- You want maximum protection
- You've experienced identity issues before

A credit freeze:

- Prevents new accounts
- Does not affect your score
- Can be temporarily lifted when needed

It's one of the strongest defensive moves available.

Why Alerts Reduce Anxiety (Not Increase It)

When set correctly:

- You stop wondering if something's wrong
- You trust your systems
- You respond instead of panic

Awareness replaces fear.

The Takeaway

Credit monitoring and alerts don't protect your credit by themselves—you do. But they give you the visibility to act fast, correct mistakes, and stop problems before they grow.

In the next section, we'll build on this with an annual credit report review checklist—a simple once-a-year habit that catches what alerts often miss and keeps your credit clean long-term.

11.2 Annual Credit Report Review Checklist

If credit monitoring is your smoke detector, your annual credit report review is your full home inspection. It's slower, more thorough, and catches problems alerts often miss. And yes—after 20 years in this field, I can tell you that most serious credit issues I've seen were caught during routine reviews, not emergencies.

This is not something you do every week. It's something you do once a year, on purpose, without distractions.

Think of it as preventative maintenance for your financial life.

Why an Annual Review Still Matters (Even with Monitoring)

- Monitoring tells you when something changes.
- An annual review tells you whether everything makes sense.

You're looking for:

- Errors that never triggered alerts
- Inconsistencies across bureaus
- Old negatives that should have fallen off
- Quiet reporting mistakes that drag scores down

These issues don't announce themselves. You have to go find them.

When to Do Your Annual Review

Pick a predictable time:

- Same month every year

- After major life events
- Before applying for major credit

Put it on your calendar. Future you will thank you.

Step 1: Pull All Three Credit Reports

Do not rely on just one bureau.

You want:

- One report from each bureau
- Side-by-side comparison if possible
- Full reports, not summaries

Different bureaus often show different problems.

Step 2: Verify Personal Information

This seems boring—and it matters.

Check:

- Name spelling
- Current and previous addresses
- Employment listings
- Social Security number accuracy (partial)

Incorrect personal data can:

- Cause mixed files
- Trigger denials
- Create identity confusion

Fix these early.

Step 3: Review Every Account Line by Line

Yes, every one.

For each account, confirm:

- It belongs to you
- Balance is correct
- Status is accurate
- Payment history matches reality
- Open or closed status is correct

If you don't recognize it, flag it immediately.

Step 4: Check Dates Carefully (This Is Huge)

Dates control everything.

Verify:

- Date opened
- Date of first delinquency
- Last reported date
- Estimated removal date for negatives

Incorrect dates can illegally extend damage.

This is one of the most common—and fixable—issues.

Step 5: Look for Duplicate or Re-Aged Accounts

Watch for:

- Same debt listed multiple times
- Original account plus collection reporting incorrectly
- Accounts with updated delinquency dates

Old debt doesn't get new life just because it was sold again.

Step 6: Review Negative Items with Fresh Eyes

For each negative item, ask:

- Is this accurate?
- Is this still allowed to report?
- Has its impact decreased?
- Is it worth disputing now?

Some negatives age quietly. Others don't belong anymore.

Step 7: Scan for Inquiry Errors

Hard inquiries should be:

- Authorized
- Accurate
- Timely

Unauthorized or outdated inquiries should be disputed.

One or two won't wreck your credit—but errors add up.

Step 8: Confirm Closed Accounts Are Reporting Correctly

Closed doesn't mean ignored.

Check that closed accounts:

- Show zero balances
- Are marked “closed by consumer” when applicable
- Aren’t reporting new activity

Closed accounts still affect your credit profile.

Step 9: Document Everything You Find

Keep:

- Notes
- Screenshots
- Dates
- Dispute plans

You don’t need to fix everything at once—but you do need a record.

Memory fades. Paper trails don’t.

Step 10: Take Action Strategically

After reviewing:

- Dispute legitimate errors
- Leave accurate aging negatives alone
- Follow up on previous disputes
- Adjust credit strategies if needed

This is not about cleaning everything—it’s about correcting what’s wrong.

A Common Mistake to Avoid

People rush.

They skim, panic, dispute everything, and create more problems than they solve.

Slow review. Targeted action. Better results.

How Long This Should Take

Plan for:

- 60–90 minutes once a year

That's it.

Ninety minutes to protect years of progress is a fair trade.

The Takeaway

An annual credit report review is one of the highest-return habits you can build. It catches silent errors, prevents long-term damage, and keeps your credit profile clean and accurate.

In the next section, we'll focus on protecting yourself from identity theft—because the best credit profile in the world won't help if someone else starts using your name.

11.3 Protecting Yourself from Identity Theft

Identity theft isn't dramatic most of the time. It's not a movie scene where someone drains your bank account overnight. It's quieter than that—and that's what makes it dangerous. After 20 years in this field, I can tell you the worst identity theft cases aren't discovered because something exploded. They're discovered because someone finally looked.

By then, the damage is already baked into the credit report.

Protecting yourself from identity theft is not about paranoia. It's about reducing exposure, limiting damage, and reacting fast when something slips through—because something eventually will.

What Identity Theft Actually Looks Like in Real Life

Most identity theft involves:

- Credit cards opened without your knowledge
- Utility or phone accounts you never authorized
- Medical billing fraud
- Address changes you didn't request
- Old accounts being taken over quietly

It's rarely obvious. It's usually discovered through:

- Credit monitoring alerts
- Annual credit report reviews
- Loan denials that don't make sense

That's why systems matter more than instincts.

Why Rebuilders Are Targeted More Often

This part isn't talked about enough.

People rebuilding credit are often more vulnerable because:

- Their information may have circulated during past financial stress
- Old accounts were sold or transferred multiple times
- They monitor less during rebuilding fatigue
- Fraud hides more easily in already-damaged reports

Strong credit profiles aren't immune—but rebuilding profiles are easier to exploit quietly.

The Single Most Powerful Protection: Credit Freezes

If you're not actively applying for credit, a credit freeze is your best defense.

A freeze:

- Prevents new accounts from being opened
- Does not affect your credit score
- Can be temporarily lifted when needed
- Stops most fraud instantly

This alone prevents the majority of identity-based credit damage.

Freezes don't stop existing account fraud—but they block new ones.

Fraud Alerts: Helpful but Limited

Fraud alerts add a note to your credit file asking lenders to verify identity.

They:

- Last for a set period
- Do not block credit entirely
- Rely on lenders actually checking

They're better than nothing—but weaker than freezes.

If you've already experienced identity theft, freezes are the better option.

Protect the Information That Gets Stolen Most Often

Identity theft usually starts with boring data.

Protect:

- Social Security number
- Date of birth
- Old addresses
- Login credentials
- Email accounts tied to financial services

Email security matters more than people realize. Many fraud cases begin with email access—not credit reports.

Use Unique Passwords for Financial Accounts

This is not optional anymore.

Best practices:

- Unique passwords for banks and credit apps
- Password manager if needed
- Two-factor authentication everywhere available

One compromised password should not unlock your entire financial life.

Watch for These Red Flags

Act immediately if you see:

- Accounts you don't recognize
- Address changes you didn't request
- Hard inquiries you didn't authorize
- Bills or collection notices out of nowhere
- Denials that don't match your profile

Delay turns small fraud into long-term cleanup.

What to Do the Moment You Suspect Identity Theft

Do not wait. Do not "see if it fixes itself."

Immediate steps:

- Freeze your credit
- Pull all three reports
- Document everything
- Dispute fraudulent accounts
- File an identity theft report if needed

Speed limits damage more than perfection.

Why Documentation Is Your Best Weapon

Identity theft resolution is paperwork-heavy.

Keep:

- Copies of disputes
- Dates of contact
- Confirmation numbers
- Screenshots
- Case references

The more organized you are, the faster resolution happens.

Identity Theft Protection Services: Worth It?

These services:

- Do not prevent theft
- Can help with monitoring and recovery
- Vary widely in quality

They can be useful if:

- You don't want to manage alerts yourself
- You've already experienced identity theft
- You value guided resolution support

They are not substitutes for freezes or awareness.

A Common Mistake That Extends Damage

People delay action because:

- They're unsure
- They don't want to overreact
- They assume it's an error

Fraud thrives on hesitation.

If it turns out to be a mistake, fine. If it's not, early action saves months of cleanup.

The Takeaway

Identity theft protection isn't about fear—it's about friction. The harder you make it for someone to misuse your information, the less damage they can do. And when something slips through, fast action keeps a bad situation from becoming a long-term credit nightmare.

In the next section, we'll focus on smart credit habits to maintain high scores—the day-to-day behaviors that quietly protect everything you've rebuilt.

11.4 Smart Credit Habits to Maintain High Scores

Once your credit score is high, the game changes. You're no longer trying to fix damage—you're trying to avoid creating new damage. And after 20 years in this field, I can tell you this is where people get careless. Not because they're irresponsible, but because success creates complacency.

High credit scores aren't maintained through effort. They're maintained through habits. Quiet ones. Boring ones. The kind you barely think about—until you stop doing them.

Let's lock these in.

The Mindset Shift That Protects High Scores

When your score improves, stop thinking:

- "I fixed my credit."

Start thinking:

- "I'm managing risk."

Credit scoring is not a reward system. It's a risk assessment tool. Your job is to continue looking boring and predictable to lenders.

Predictable people get the best terms.

Habit #1: Automate Minimum Payments Forever

Even when money is abundant, autopay stays on.

Every account:

- Minimum payment

- Autopay enabled
- Backed by a funded account

Manual payments are optional. Protection is not.

This one habit prevents more score damage than anything else.

Habit #2: Keep Utilization Boring

High scorers don't flirt with limits.

Best practice:

- Let one card report a small balance
- Keep others near zero
- Avoid spikes near statement close

You don't need to micromanage—but you do need awareness.

Habit #3: Respect Statement Closing Dates

You don't have to live by them—but you need to know them.

People with strong scores:

- Pay early when balances grow
- Time large purchases strategically
- Avoid surprises on reports

This keeps utilization from quietly creeping up.

Habit #4: Don't Open Credit Out of Boredom

One of the fastest ways to hurt a strong profile is unnecessary applications.

Avoid opening accounts because:

- You were approved
- There was a bonus
- It felt harmless

Every new account adds:

- Inquiry impact
- Average age reduction
- Risk signals

Strong credit thrives on stability, not activity.

Habit #5: Review Reports Even When Things Are "Fine"

High scorers check credit not because they expect problems—but because they don't want surprises.

Annual reviews catch:

- Silent errors
- Misreported balances
- Unauthorized changes
- Old negatives that should have dropped

Confidence comes from verification, not assumption.

Habit #6: Maintain a Cash Buffer

High credit scores often coexist with low stress because:

- Emergencies don't turn into missed payments
- Credit cards aren't emergency funds

- Cash flow stays predictable

A buffer protects credit more than discipline ever could.

Habit #7: Address Issues Immediately

High scorers don't ignore small problems.

If:

- A payment fails
- A balance spikes
- An alert triggers

They act quickly.

Small issues handled fast rarely become credit problems.

Habit #8: Keep Old Accounts Open (When Sensible)

Length of history matters.

If an account:

- Has no annual fee
- Isn't tempting overspending
- Is well-managed

Keeping it open often helps more than closing it.

Age is an asset.

Habit #9: Use Credit as a Tool, Not a Crutch

This is subtle—but important.

Healthy credit behavior looks like:

- Spending what you can pay
- Paying balances quickly
- Using credit for convenience, not necessity

When credit stops being emotional, scores stay high.

The Quiet Reality of Excellent Credit

People with excellent credit:

- Don't think about credit often
- Don't chase points
- Don't react emotionally to fluctuations

They let systems do the work.

A Common Way High Scores Get Lost

People celebrate, relax, and stop paying attention.

Then:

- One late payment happens
- One balance creeps up
- One account gets ignored

Momentum doesn't protect you—habits do.

The Takeaway

Maintaining high credit scores isn't about vigilance—it's about design. When you build habits that default to protection, your credit stays strong with minimal effort.

In the final section, we'll zoom out and talk about teaching financial literacy to the next generation—because the best credit strategy of all is making sure these mistakes don't have to be relearned.

11.5 Teaching Financial Literacy to the Next Generation

If I could go back 20 years and change one thing about my own financial life, it wouldn't be a missed payment or a bad loan—it would be learning how credit actually works earlier. Most of us didn't fail because we were reckless. We failed because nobody explained the rules before handing us the game.

That's why this chapter matters. Teaching financial literacy to the next generation isn't about making kids obsessed with money. It's about giving them context before consequences.

And no—you don't need to be a finance expert to do it right.

Why Financial Literacy Is a Credit Strategy

Credit problems are rarely about math. They're about:

- Poor expectations
- Emotional spending
- Confusion about consequences
- Lack of systems

When kids understand why things work the way they do, they make fewer costly mistakes later.

Literacy prevents damage before it happens.

Start with Concepts, Not Products

You don't begin with interest rates or credit cards.

You start with:

- Spending vs earning
- Delayed gratification
- Fixed vs flexible expenses
- Choices and tradeoffs

These ideas form the foundation for responsible credit behavior later.

Age-Appropriate Lessons That Actually Stick

For younger kids:

- Money comes from work, not magic
- Spending means choosing one thing over another
- Saving gives options later

For teens:

- How debit differs from credit
- Why borrowing isn't free
- What "on time" really means
- How mistakes follow you

You don't need lectures. You need repetition and examples.

Normalize Conversations About Money

One of the biggest mistakes parents make is treating money like a taboo subject.

When money is hidden:

- Kids fill gaps with assumptions

- Shame replaces understanding
- Mistakes become secrets

Talk openly—without fear or drama.

Teach Credit Before They're Offered It

Most people get their first credit card before they understand utilization, interest, or reporting.

Flip that script.

Before they apply, explain:

- How balances are reported
- Why minimum payments are traps
- How interest compounds
- Why late payments linger

Knowledge before access changes everything.

Authorized User Accounts as Teaching Tools

Used thoughtfully, authorized user status can:

- Introduce credit reporting
- Build early history
- Create teachable moments

Used carelessly, it can backfire.

If you do this:

- Choose low-utilization accounts

- Set clear expectations
- Monitor activity closely

Credit education beats credit shortcuts.

Teach Systems, Not Willpower

Kids don't need motivation—they need structure.

Show them:

- Autopay
- Budgeting by paycheck
- Saving before spending
- Using alerts and reminders

Systems protect people when emotions don't.

Mistakes Are Part of Learning (Within Limits)

Sheltering kids from all financial mistakes doesn't help.

Let them:

- Miss a small opportunity
- Feel the sting of a bad choice
- Learn recovery in low-risk environments

Guided failure builds competence.

Model the Behavior You Want Them to Learn

This is uncomfortable—but true.

Kids learn more from what you do than what you say.

If you:

- Panic about bills
- Avoid money conversations
- Treat credit emotionally

They absorb that.

Model calm, structured behavior instead.

Break the Cycle Intentionally

Many families pass down financial stress, not because they want to—but because no one stopped to explain things differently.

You can be the interruption.

Teaching financial literacy is one of the most impactful generational gifts you can give.

The Takeaway

Credit knowledge isn't just about higher scores—it's about fewer regrets. When the next generation understands money before it becomes powerful in their lives, they don't need to recover from the same mistakes.

That concludes Repair Your Credit: Remove Errors, Pay Down Debt, Rebuild Score. If there's one theme throughout this book, it's this: credit isn't about perfection—it's about understanding the system well enough to work with it instead of against it.

You're not behind. You're informed. And that changes everything.

www.ingramcontent.com/pod-product-compliance
Lightning Source LLC
LaVergne TN
LVHW052036200926
848481LV00005B/1700